Morning Messages

Invitations

your actions make A
difference

Blessings of gRatitude

Peggy Black

Morning Messages Invitations

Written by Peggy Black in partnership with the 'team'
(Original art and text Copyright © 2007 Library of Congress USA)
Copyright © 2010 by Peggy Black All Rights Reserved

Book and Cover Design, Graphics:
Peggy Black and Melanie Gendron

Melanie Gendron
Gendron Studios
P. O. Box 1438
Felton, CA. 95018
www.melaniegendron.com
gentarot@comcast.net
831-335-9064

Publisher: Motivational Press, Inc
7668 El Camino Real #104-223
Carlsbad, CA 92009
www.MotivationalPress.com

Peggy Black: Transducer, Scribe and Witness
Executive Producer, Cover Design, Transmissions, Drawings
Morning Messages, P. O. Box 199, Felton, CA. 95018
www.morningmessages.com
joyandgratitude@aol.com
831-335-3145

ISBN: 978-1-935723-11-0

Manufactured in the United States of America

Testimonies from Readers...

I thought you would enjoy knowing that a friend of mine who owns a state wide office and after receiving messages the first week, she addressed all 80 members of her staff to subscribe and read your morning messages at the beginning of their work day. — Nancy

YOU do indeed make a giant difference in my life and all for the better! — Barry

Hi, Dave here, you have no idea how much all this is helping me develop myself. I can not describe in words how grateful I am.

I am separated from my husband, moved to a busy city and registered for college. I sometimes feel alone and vulnerable...the city is frightening and my studies can be difficult. Some days I just want to curl up and go back to bed. Your messages help, uplift and inspire me to continue. — Love, Mary

There are long periods in my life in which I was very depressed, but reading these messages makes me realize that it is important to live here and be sure to be positive in life. — Fia, the Netherlands

The Morning Messages, have provided much solace and peace for me. — Thanks, Peter

My friend Nancy's husband is dealing with Stage IV cancer — says that the Morning Messages have been their rock — that Eric reads them every day and receives immense benefit. She says that words from them come back to her throughout her days and give her comfort and inspirations. Thank you for what you are doing. — Jane

I am going through a divorce after 29 years with 2 teenage boys and your messages are so positive and helping me let go of the negativity. I love the thought of radiating love, joy and appreciation. — Joan

I don't know what it means, but as soon as I saw the drawings, I started crying, tears are flowing still as I put my hand on the computer screen to touch the drawings. — Thank you so much, Jennie

I delight in receiving your messages. They make perfect sense and are a welcome reminder. — Blessings, Chris — New Zealand

The messages keep me striving to make daily choices that raise my frequency such that I can exude source energy and support all I come in contact with throughout the day. Thanks for your effort in making this world an environment we choose to co-create as more peaceful, kind and forgiving. — Gratitude, Kevin

Your story, the movie and the message brought tears to my eyes. It is exactly the right answer to my prayers. — Wilka — the Netherlands

Hello Peggy, your work is helping so many of us remember to turn within and ask for guidance and inspiration. We do not realize what assistance is so available to us. You make that a real presence for us. I love your playful, prayerful, simplistic approach. Your messages bring joy and lightness. — Namaste, Rev. Sherran

How much I have been fighting with myself, with the world, with the whole universe lately. How grateful I now feel for these messages. — Kaarina — Finland

Many many thanks to you and your guide friends for sharing your love. Each message moves energy within me to a higher frequency… I CANNOT EXPRESS ENOUGH GRATITUDE. — Love, Jerry

I am learning late in my life about receiving gifts of joy and truly coming from higher vibrations that can radiate to others. I have received your messages through a portal that I never knew existed within me. It is now a part of me. Deep gratitude for your words, your spirit, your sharing. — Terry

Thank you so much for talking about fear. I just went through a situation where fear was keeping me imbalanced and unconscious. You put it so clearly that I could see how I let FEAR control me and made me lose sight of me. — Vicky

It is so wonderful, the gift you bring to us. It gives me a great excuse to trust the universe a little bit more and to risk a little bit more love to people. — Light, Dharma — Philippines

Hello, my name is Klaus and I am from Austria, but my English is not perfect. There is so much truth in your writing, somehow this are no teachings… this are words that let you resonate your own truth within.

Praise for the Invitations...

Whenever I find myself mentally stuck in a negative place... I read or listen to the Morning Messages; they always offer me a shift in consciousness that I welcome. — Thank you for your work, Thomas

A very powerful invitation, very clear instructions. I did the work, and the issue began to clear. Lead me right through the process to a resolution. It was a wondrous shift for me. WOW, a miraculous change! — Tina

Whenever you are feeling uncertain with a quality of your essence or life direction, Morning Messages Invitations, offers profound insights you can embrace in your "power of now"- supporting new possibilities! — Leigh Wunce, NC, Medical Intuitive

I love my Morning Message invitations, before I open my computer or have coffee, I take a moment and read the message, I am amazed by the drawings, they make me smile and feel good instantly! The invitation reminds me to focus on the good that surrounds me with such abundance. Awesome!! — Gabriella

These Morning Message invitations are phenomenal! They are a wonderful resource for me to feel inspired, grounded, expanded, illuminated, encouraged, and comforted. They are always a perfect match to my experiences and needs, a guiding light in my ever blossoming journey. — Michelle — Honolulu, Hawai'i

Having a home office allows me easy access to the Morning Messages Invitations throughout my day. This is a lovely combination of the wisdom of the Morning Messages and my own creative work. — Blessings, Ellen

I gifted two dear friends with your Morning Message Invitation deck. THEY ARE BEAUTIFUL! We did a ceremony and blessed the deck, and each drew a card. We all felt the presence of "your team." We ended up touching, reading and holding each one to our hearts. We were in such a sacred space. — Love you, Lida

I am recovering from breast cancer, and I plan to include the Morning Messages Invitation deck in my series. I am teaching other women on how to BE A STAR in their own lives. — Raywyn

I keep my Morning Messages invitations by my bed. I choose one to read and study. I feel blessed to enjoy such treasures for my dreams! Thank you so much for your creations, Peggy. — Judy — Guatemala

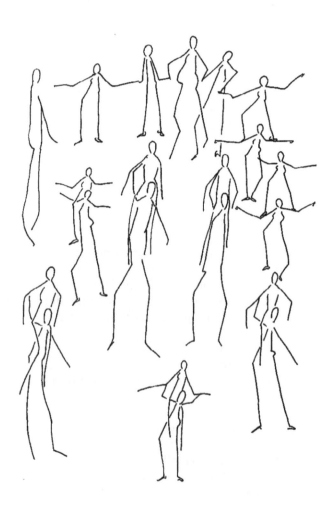

Gratitudes and Appreciation...

It has been an honor to bring Morning Messages, "We Are Here" Transmissions to the global community.

I have been privileged to experience the blessings, and miracles that have embraced every aspect of the process. Each step of this path has offered support and connection that has truly been inspiring.

I especially thank the subscribers, the readers of the Morning Messages. As a result of your sharing, the Morning Messages family has over 10,000 global members, and each day there are new subscribers. I am grateful for your support with the expansion of this work and these words. Your letters and correspondence continue to enrich my life. It is a delight to read how the messages from the 'team' touch you and inspire your remembrance of who you are.

It was my privilege to connect with you on a personal level through the private channeled readings. I am uplifted by your courage and strength as you have shared your life experiences. I am grateful to witness your extraordinary abilities and gifts that you personally bring to the collective, to your community and to your family.

I thank you for your donations — they always arrived in amazingly perfect timing to meet a financial need. It is with deep appreciation to those who sponsored the website, the invitation deck and the two books. Each time I extended an invitation and request for financial support, it was forthcoming immediately. It is in true partnership that these offerings and products were made manifest. May your generosity be multiplied a thousandfold.

I honor with joy and gratitude a very special team of friends and family who have gifted me their support, time and encouragement, and whose efforts were acknowledged in the companion book, The Morning Messages "We Are Here" Transmissions.

I am grateful for my deep connection to Divine Source in all its manifestations. I am grateful for "my team" who continue to offer their love, wisdom and guidance reminding me to stay in my heart.

"All success in life comes from the generous support and love of our friends." —blessings of grace and joy, Peggy

Dedication

It is an honor to dedicate this book
to the incredible individuals
who are touched by these invitations
from Morning Messages and
who continue to offer their conscious actions
to make a difference in our world.

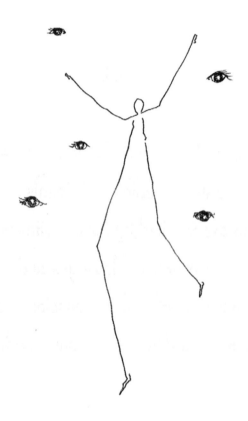

Wisdom and Guidelines
For Multidimensional Humans

Know that it is your birthright to awaken.

With a gentle heart, love yourself free
of all imagined limitations.

Remember, the important key is in the asking and the
willingness. State your intentions and surrender.

You are a vibrational being;
practice raising your vibrations with each breath.

Always ask yourself if this word, action or emotion
is life-diminishing or life-enhancing.

You are here to transmute and transform energy
through the alchemical chalice of your heart.

Practice simple, dedicated actions
infused with your joy, gratitude, appreciation.

By placing your awareness in your heart,
you naturally dwell in the synchronicities of now.

Each time you shift an emotional response
from anger or judgment to love, joy or gratitude,
you are doing global service work on a personal level.

Your sacred heart space is the gateway to all awareness,
well-being and the oneness with all.
It is your link to the cosmic grid
and your way home.

Honor your total, magnificent, multidimensional Self.

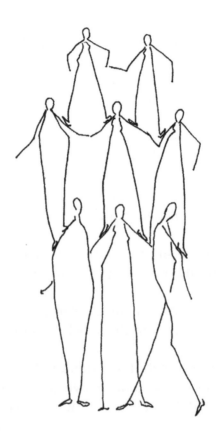

Morning Messages
Invitations

Wisdom and Guidance for Multidimensional Humans

by Peggy Black
in partnership with the 'team'

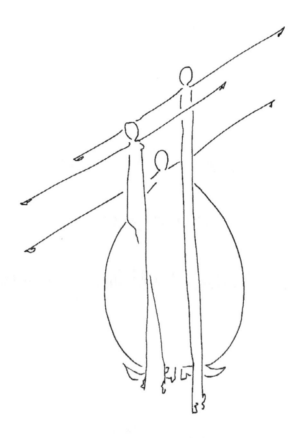

Contents...

Morning Messages Invitations...

Monthly Transmissions from the 'team'...

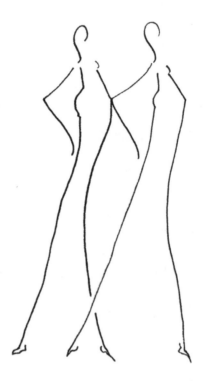

Foreward...

It is time to stretch beyond your knowing, to access that deeper part of yourself, and awaken the multidimensional being that you are.

In this companion book to *The Morning Messages: "We Are Here" Transmissions*, Peggy Black, Sacred Sound Salutarist, Spiritual Synergist, Transducer and Scribe, shares the practices that have been downloaded to her by her celestial team so that you may shift from your current state of reality and begin to allow another more delicious reality to emerge in your life.

The exercises that are provided in the *Morning Message Invitations* will enable you to open your circuits to receive clearer guidance from your own celestial team. As you read the *Morning Message Invitations* each day, you will learn how to access a greater field of possibilities and anchor much higher and more coherent frequencies of joy, abundance and harmony.

The *Morning Message Invitations* are your daily call to conscious action. Let them be a reminder that by engaging in the right kinds of conscious practices, you can transform your life — and even help shift consciousness on the planet!

It is time for each of us to step up and participate in this grand awakening. I am delighted to witness this unfolding as thousands of us join with Peggy to embrace these messages and do our part to add more light to the planet.

May you be blessed and transformed by these magnificent invitations.

— Randy Peyser, author of *The Power of Miracle Thinking*

Every Time...

W e are here. It is our desire to share these messages and offer an invitation for humans to establish a strong link and awareness to the many aspects of their own multidimensional reality. Each individual who awakens to the knowing that they are multidimensional starhumans contributes to the whole.

It is important for humans to realize that they travel from one dimension to another many times a day. Remember you only see what you believe. Reality will match your beliefs. The dimensions are a matter of frequency and vibration. This truth is becoming known to many on your planet.

It is the awareness and the welcoming that allow for the merging and the exchange between our frequency and vibration and your frequency and vibration. We invite you to allow the softening and the merging of the dimensions. Let there be a flow, gentle and smooth.

It is a matter of shifting frequency and vibration. The most powerful tool in this hologame on earth, the golden key so to speak, is the conscious practice and skill at holding a pure frequency of joy, gratitude and appreciation no matter what is happening. Continue to return to the alchemical chalice of the heart and radiate these vibrations into your daily life, moment-to-moment-to-moment.

These are incredible times upon your planet. There is a shift in the matrix that is taking place. Humanity is experiencing considerable changes in perceived reality. You have always been straddling multi-realties — the shift that is happening now is that you are awakening and becoming conscious that you are doing it. You are aware of your physical surroundings, those frozen in your perception, and you are also aware of the information we are offering — that with very little effort you can travel to any location in the galaxy.

Your human body is always operating in multi-realities. Every cell is aware of the noise within the body and outside the body and is making the necessary adjustments. Every cell of the body is reading the position of the sun, moon, and stars and making the necessary adjustments. Every cell of the body is monitoring all input from all dimensions and making the necessary adjustments. Every cell of the body operates at a multidimensional level and knowing.

Humans are evolving and becoming conscious that they are affecting the reality that they step into, and they are affecting the movement of energy on the planet. As they stand fully engaged and mindful of the total connection... the total matrix of divine unfolding... the total oneness and total weaving with the All That Is, they are starhumans.

This evolution is occurring within the atoms of each human being on earth at this time.

There is, and has been, a vanguard of multidimensional starhumans who have been carrying this banner of enlightenment for lifetimes. There is an awakening to the knowledge that each human is multidimensional. Now is the time to recognize and merge with the consciousness of others who are also cognizant of their multidimensional beingness.

As humans begin to expand into their multidimensional aspects, they will become pioneers in aligning, balancing and untangling the energy weavings. There is a restoring and mending of the grid of this planet. This work has been taking place for hundreds of years in the subtle realms. It is now taking place in the active physical realms. This restoring, this mending of the grid, is held in the galactic realms. This is the time, the coming together. This shift is activating your very purpose to serve.

There are considerable numbers of others like you who recognize their purpose in this evolution of consciousness that is taking place. They have reached out requesting assistance and support on this stage of physical reality. Their conscious request has been heard, and much is being offered from the convergence of the highest vibrations in the universe.

We invite you and other awakened humans to hold the focus and anchor these energetic gifts that are being showered upon you. With every breath you take, realize that you are Light, you are needed, and it is time for you to be fully awake. Your every vibration, your every thought, is projected into the matrix of the energy field of planet earth. Continue to ask yourself, "Does this word, thought, action, feeling add to the dysfunction of the world, or does it add to the light of the world?"

Remember, you are an important part of this unfolding. Each starhuman carries a code that triggers this realization in the other. Each encounter holds the auspicious moment in which codes and activation take place between both beings. When you are vibrating at your highest and most inspired frequency, this is when the opening is available to lift any lower vibrations within another human.

Every time a multidimensional starhuman makes a conscious choice to experience an uplifted thought, a high frequency vibration of joy, gratitude or appreciation, there is a shift in the entire matrix of humanity. Every time.

Every time that a multidimensional starhuman stretches to be more compassionate, more understanding, more authentic there is a shift in the entire matrix of humanity. Every time.

Every time you and others anchor this frequency, this truth, this knowing; when you vibrate the high resonance of joy, gratitude, appreciation, you welcome and allow others to connect with their own awareness of their multidimensional magnificence. Every time.

One by one, humans are stepping into their mastery, their authority, and their personal sovereignty. We are celebrating with you in this incredible shift that is taking place. We invite you to stay the course, walk the path, and share who you are with others from this high, expanded multidimensional starhuman place.

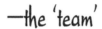

—the 'team'

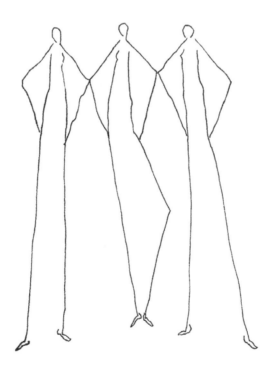

Living the Invitations...

The Morning Messages Invitations is a companion book. Its purpose and goal is to be the book that you reach for when you need clarity, guidance, or a shift in your perceptions. Not only is it your companion, it is also the partner and companion of the *Morning Messages "We Are Here" Transmissions* book. Each of these books stands proudly on its own, offering reminders of our power, as well as our magnificence. Together, however, they weave a framework of words that can and will expand your awareness and consciousness, in a playful and simple manner.

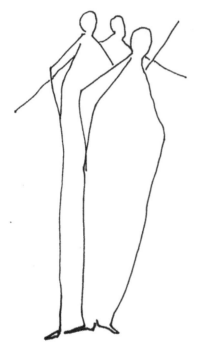

It was in 2005 that I first became acquainted with the transmissions through a group that I call my 'team'. It seems that I was able to translate, transduce, their energy to bring their ideas and expanded concepts into form. My life has certainly changed since they became my friends and I began hanging around with these transmissions and invitations. The transmissions were made available on the Morning Messages website where thousands and thousands have now read them. These messages are available on CDs, and they are also offered in a special guidance deck of forty-four invitations which empower and honor your multidimensional self.

These forty-four invitations are now gracing the pages of the book you hold in your hand. I want you to know that these are not just any invitations—these are special. They are small aspects of the much larger transmissions. Yet, do not let their size disarm you. They are powerful. They are the active aspects

24

of the concepts. Each invitation will encourage you to practice a shift in consciousness, to widen, lengthen, broaden and deepen the way that you are viewing the experiences of your day. When you accept their courteous requests, and begin to put into action their suggestions, they will change your life. Your life will change in amazing, incredible ways. So I am giving you a heads up on this one.

I speak from experience since I have been engaged with these transmissions and invitations for the last several years. These concepts, ideas and suggestions have truly been my companions. I apply the methods and use the energetic tools for personal issues in my life, and I can attest to their power in achieving results.

These simple exercises can be incorporated into everything that you do; in fact, that is what these invitations are all about. With them come the awareness and the realization that you are influencing the energy fields around you. You are influencing the results. You are the master key to what is happening in your life. You also have an effective role in shifting the collective dysfunctions in society and in the world.

Since I began using these invitations, these conscious exercises in my daily life, I have witnessed and observed a shift in the outcomes of situations I was experiencing. On a personal level, I appreciate the grace, the miracles and the synchronicities that have been occurring in my life. Now when they do not occur, I wonder what and where I could have shifted.

There is another section in this book that offers more in depth transmissions. They are clear in their messages; in every encounter we have, we can offer the gift of an uplifting, emotional blessing. My partnership with the 'team' has continued to encourage me to realize and own that I have a responsibility to consciously interact with each energy field I encounter. Their suggestions are always in the moment, appropriate to the event or activity.

I remember the first time this occurred. I was waiting for my plane to depart, reading and totally unaware of my surroundings. I received an energetic tap on the shoulder from my 'team' with the question, *"Do you realize you could enhance and bless this energy field?"*

Once I heard this request, I put the book down, and began to focus my awareness in my heart, where I allowed the feeling of gratitude and appreciation to swell. I imagined this wave of gratitude and appreciation radiating out from my heart like ripples upon the water. This coherent vibration created by my true feeling of gratitude was being added to the collective energy field of the airport.

The 'team' inquired if I would like to witness how my wave of coherent vibration of gratitude had touched the energy fields of others. Instantly, upon the screen of my inner vision, I was shown a very frustrated mother traveling with several small fussy children. As the coherent wave of gratitude rippled by this weary group of travelers, I witnessed the tired mother relax her shoulders and sigh, the children quieted in their restlessness, the crying stopped. It was a profound experience for me to see the effects of my conscious offering.

Next the 'team' showed me a couple sitting very rigid and stiff in their grief. As this wave of coherent energy moved past them, they relaxed and leaned into one another for comfort and solace, touching hands. I was moved to tears to realize that my simple act of conscious kindness had shifted the energy field of these individuals.

We are always impacting the energy fields we interface with in our daily activities. We are not passive, quietly moving from place to place, store to store, or activity to activity. You might say we leave a trail of our energy vibrations everywhere. The question to ask yourself is — are the energy traces you are offering to any collective field depressing or uplifting? Are you adding a vibration of stress, fear and judgment, or are you adding a coherent frequency of joy, gratitude and appreciation?

This is where you truly claim your personal power; with the awareness that you are always adding to the energy matrix, you always have the opportunity to make a conscious difference. It actually becomes a very fun exercise. Like any exercise, the more you practice the better you get. Offering your "conscious energy" becomes a positive action that you incorporate into your life.

The Morning Messages invitations and transmissions are simple reminders that will assist you in daily exercises to offer a higher, coherent vibration in all your encounters and activities. Have fun, express yourself in unique ways that are yours alone, add to the blessings and the uplifting of energy everywhere you travel.

These invitations are only a beginning. Once you recognize your own personal power to transform what is before you, you will be unstoppable.

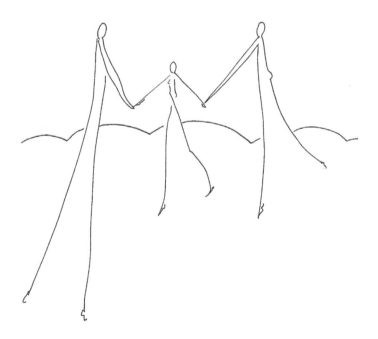

No RSVP Required...

The Morning Messages invitations in this book can be used as a daily oracle, or daily guide, in practicing the shifting of your beliefs and actions throughout the day. This is an inner-active book. Its use will become a powerful exercise of expanded consciousness. Each invitation will request, will entice, and will summon you to step into new ways of responding to your life, to events and to others.

Once you begin using these suggestions, these invitations, there will be no turning back. Your life will change, your life will transform. You will begin to expect miracles every day. You will begin to notice the incredible synchronicities that seem to manifest in every phase of your life. You will be amazed that you are creating awesome realities.

You will realize the incredible opportunity that is offered to you, and you will lighten up. You will begin to enjoy yourself no matter what is happening in your life. You will have the awesome tools and gifts to shift your response in a quantum moment. You will be free and in your joy, living in the presence of your sacred heart, fulfilled and alive, expressing who you truly are.

This book also contains more advanced transmissions for those who want to delve deeper. These were offered in a monthly newsletter to the more than 10,000 subscribers of the Morning Messages website. They are powerful, thought provoking energy changing downloads of information. You will recognize and begin to honor your magnificence and own your power as a multidimensional being. You will begin to understand why you are here in this hologame on planet earth.

I invite you to open your mind and heart to these invitations and transmissions that are touching so many individuals around the world during these changing times.

Morning Messages
Invitations

consciousness exercises which support
and call forth your powerful,
authentic and magnificent Self

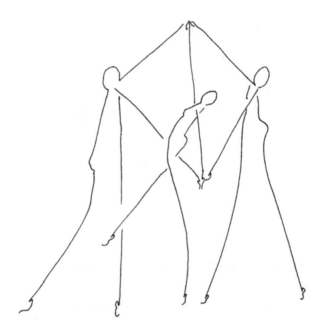

Feel us in your heart...

We Offer Our Guidance

We have supported the evolution of humanity and your planet for eons, with our heart's love and energetic radiance.

We dwell in a higher energy frequency and field than your personal energy signature, yet just as you are, we are also ascending into the One Source, the All That Is.

We are your celestial, energetic team, your intergalactic, interdimensional heart family, your starry brethren, we offer our love and support, as you awaken and remember your magnificence and your own multidimensional Starself.

We offer our guidance upon your request.

We join you as partners in the space of your sacred heart. When your energy signature is one of the coherent emotions of joy, gratitude, love, appreciation and compassion it is a match to our frequency.

Feel us in your heart and sing your sound and songs of joy and gratitude. We will meet you there.

Soften the grip of your limited self.

You are Invited to Wake Up

There is an energetic, evolutionary wave that is occurring in the psyche of all earth dwellers. The aspect of you that knows the grand truth is awakening to the awareness that you are a magnificent, expanded, multidimensional being.

In order to embrace any aspect of your multidimensional self, you're invited to release the hold of the ego patterns and limitations. You're invited to wake up.

When you practice holding a clear vibration of joy, gratitude and appreciation, you begin to soften the grip of the ego mind.

When you bless rather than judge, when you place your awareness in your heart, you are softening the grip of your limited self.

Each conscious act is a step closer to your authentic, magnificent self and the realms of unlimited wonder.

We invite you to take these conscious steps, and relax, knowing that you are loved and all is well.

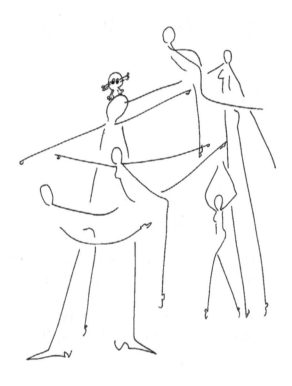

Practice the awareness of joy...

Joy

Joy is a state of mind; it is a vibration unlike any other. Joy is an emotional sense of being... simply that.

Humans have been programmed to believe that there must be a reason to be joyful, and those reasons are often fleeting and brief.

The concept of constantly radiating joy is a bit difficult for some to imagine, especially when you have so much to "worry" about.

We invite you to sense and welcome joy. Let yourself examine the feeling of joy. When are you filled with joy? What are the conditions or situations?

Practice the awareness of joy, being in the vibration, the feeling and the emotion of joy. When you hold a joy vibration instead of fear or worry, you are in a position of powerful creating.

You are open and receptive to your blessings.

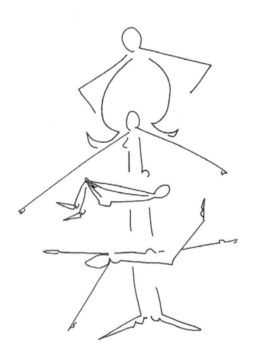

A ritual honors the moment.

Ritual

Your every action is holy. Create rituals that honor and enhance the stages of the day. A morning ritual can be as simple as a spoken prayer.

Light a candle, bring your awareness fully into your body, and fill yourself with the gift of the morning's energy and sounds. It is a time for gratitude, a time for intention, a time to connect.

Then, at your mid-day, you have entered another stage; leave behind what is complete from the morning and step into this different rhythm and energy.

Do this again at twilight as the sun gives way to the stars. Before your night's sleep, perform a ritual to honor the day lived, acknowledging self, releasing all that needs to be released. This is an opportunity to offer forgiveness and gratitude.

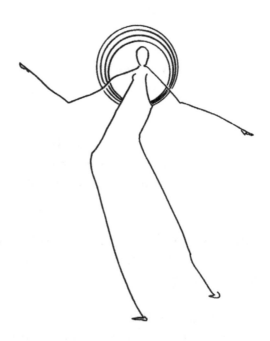

Rituals offer great power.

Creating Ritual

Rituals open and close any activity or time frame. Become aware of the rituals already in your life; see how you can shift and elevate your habits to become a sacred act.

Rituals assist in the full spiritual presence coming forth.

A ritual before a meal prepares the mind/body to accept the foods offered... a prayer of gratitude... a simple bowed head... completes the act of eating.

A ritual intention created as you shower/bathe has great power to cleanse the energy field, as well as the body.

Create rituals that acknowledge the seasons and stages in your life. By honoring these passages, you step cleanly into the next. With these conscious actions, you will embody each activity and stage of your life more fully.

By the act of creating rituals, you stay more conscious, present, and alive to who you truly are.

...time to pause and reset.

Practice Stillness

We invite you to develop the skill of maintaining your personal center. Practice stillness; be quiet for a few moments several times a day. This offers a simple, quick way to reach your balance. Stillness allows your body, mind, emotions, and spirit to realign.

When you are feeling the most stressed, it is time to pause and reset. Conscious stillness keeps your circuits open for guidance; it opens the doors of awareness.

Practice breathing deeply and quieting your mind as often as needed, until it comes naturally.

Your conscious stillness offers a safe harbor... a balanced frequency for others to entrain and resonate with.

Your energy field of stillness will shift your interface with others, it will ripple outward... shifting and transforming all energy it touches. This will assist the global matrix to resonate a state of balance.

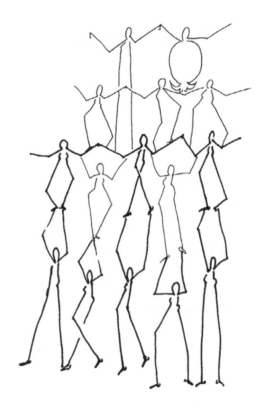

Bless another...

Conscious Kindness

We invite you to take personal responsibility for your evolution of consciousness as you observe the challenges and chaos activated by collective fear in the world.

This evolution is being supported by your celestial brethren. Ask for and allow guidance and support. Assistance is as near to you as water is to the fish.

Hold firm your resolve, knowing your divine oneness. Hold firm to the frequency of joy and gratitude.

Each time you convert a response from anger or hatred to one of kindness and acceptance you are a part of the cosmic shift of the ages.

When you bless another, rather than push against, there is a subtle shift in the collective matrix. These small acts of conscious kindness transform reality.

Be in your conscious kindness today and observe with gratitude the magic that occurs.

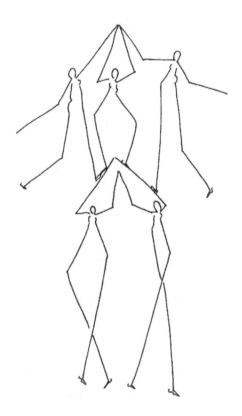

How fully conscious are you?

Flow in NOW

One of the important masteries and skills you bring to all your experiences is how fully conscious you are in each NOW.

The belief that everything is a struggle or a challenge is strong in mass consciousness. This is an illusion and a learned pattern.

Experiencing struggle or stress manifests disharmony in any activity; and it takes conscious skill to change and transform this pattern.

When your awareness is in the NOW, and your energetic stance is a high vibration, there will be a flow, a grace, and an ease.

It does not matter what you are doing, or with whom you are doing it, the key is to be in the moment, fully filled with your joy, gratitude, and appreciation.

It is not what you do, but how you do each moment.

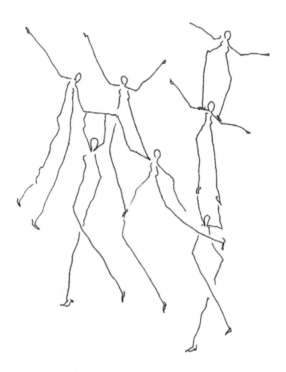

Practice being light-hearted.

Be in Joy

Joy is an elixir and healing balm. When you radiate a vibration of joy, there is a chemical shift within your body which is reflected in the response of your reality. You will bypass the usual stress of worry to a more conscious, relaxed state of mind and heart.

Joy clears the way for incredible miracles.

Smile as you answer the phone, make a meal, and pay your bills. Smile at your reflection in the mirror. Smile as you fall asleep. Smile when you think. Rejoice with your breath — smile for no reason, smile into the moment.

Imagine you have a joy muscle — stretch it, expand it and fully express it.

Laugh, giggle, radiate cheerfulness, practice being light-hearted, carefree, and elated about the blessings in your life.

Be happy, rejoice and enjoy. "BE IN JOY".

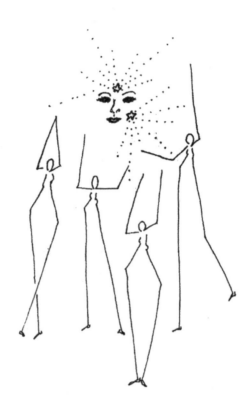

Allow yourself to receive.

Manifestant

What is it to manifest? It is to reveal, to bring into light, to embody and to materialize.

Each human carries some aspect of limiting beliefs that have been handed down from one generation to the next. Where has your thinking been programmed?

Step out of the haze of powerlessness and fear; shake off the misconceptions of lack and scarcity.

You are unlimited, infinite, and powerful beyond measure. You are a creator, an energy vortex and a manifestant of the highest degree.

Step into this knowing and awareness. Embody this true, clear power, knowing you are a multidimensional starhuman.

Scan your life; make a list, reviewing and discovering all the times you asked and did receive. Practice abundant receiving with gratitude.

Graciously allow yourself to receive what you have asked for.

Offer your full divine presence.

Dance in the NOW

There is magic and an alchemical power when you ride the wave of the NOW.

Mundane, repeated tasks become unconscious behavior. When the mind is on automatic, it easily goes to the past or future, bypassing present moment.

The mind is a spendthrift of the NOW.

Any mundane activity is an opportunity for divine transformation. Bring your presence to the activity and infuse it with your consciousness.

The simple act of taking out the trash can be infused with intention and 'light energy', so that wherever the trash goes, it shifts the energy of everything it touches.

The highest and grandest service you offer is your full divine presence in each NOW. Begin to notice the colors of the sky, the subtle sounds and textures around you.

Dance in the NOW with all your senses.

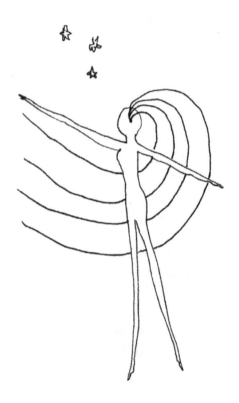

You have tools and master keys...

Call It Forward

You are a transformer, pure and simple. You have tools and master keys of energetic alchemy — the awesome ability to transform your reality from dysfunction to empowerment.

You are the cutting edge of awareness in physical form.

You are riding the energy wave of transformation, catching the wind of change in your sail, running the rapids as you envision the most delicious possibilities.

The gift of each new day is put aside as you pick up the remains of yesterday. Strive to awaken from imposed slumber.

When doubts arise, transform the emotional, mental dysfunction of feeling powerless. This transmuting of energy is an hourly, daily and lifetime process.

Play with joy and abandon. Play with wonder and skill. Dance; weave the energy fields with gratitude and appreciation.

Imagine the very best results — call it forward.

Your spirit is the force that animates...

Body Partnership

The human body is unique in the entire universe. It is a manifestation of sacred geometry, vibrations of energy and sound, held and woven together by divine intent.

Your spirit is the force that animates the body; it is an interactive partnership affected and managed by your emotions and thoughts.

When your spirit and physical body are not in clear communication, there is disharmony.

Each cell is conscious. Communicate with your body as its spiritual CEO. Learn its language and hear its subtle messages.

Be in conversation with your body.

Focus where there is tension or pain. How does this pain or tension serve you? What beliefs, thoughts or emotions are held there? Acknowledge these issues, and ask your body if it's ready to release them.

Practice appreciating your body and the dynamic gifts it offers.

Stretch, move, dance...

Physical Awareness

The human body was designed to allow you to have the utmost expression of freedom in your earthly journey, allowing your spiritual, energetic soul-self to experience the richness of this reality.

As a Being of Energy and Light embodied, you are meant to interface with this dimension fully aware and awake to your actions, thoughts and feelings.

You are the force that animates the form, which embraces physical denseness. You are divine. You are Spirit. You are a magnificent, multidimensional Being.

Since most physical movement is automatic, practice sensing the movement of your body.

Be totally present with the sensations happening in all areas of your body as you walk, stretch, move, or dance.

Be conscious in your expanded Spirit-Self, while also aware of your physical form as it moves through your activities.

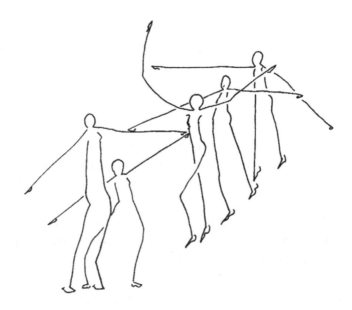

Be in your heart and transform the conflict.

Peace

You are a being of great contrast. We invite you to see the contrast, the opposites, and hold them both without judging or becoming polarized.

Peace is absent when there is inner conflict. Conflict is created when there are different beliefs within a person — when there is 'warring' within the mind and heart.

It is the ego judging that keeps both 'warring within' and 'warring without' in place. Judging holds you in its tight grip of conflict.

There is no peace in a mind that judges. Judging keeps you separate.

Peace comes when you hold the contrast in the transforming, alchemical energy of your heart awareness.

Sit quietly, with your awareness in your heart, take several deep breaths, and hold the contrast until the energy of the heart transforms the conflict. With practice, this becomes easier and more natural.

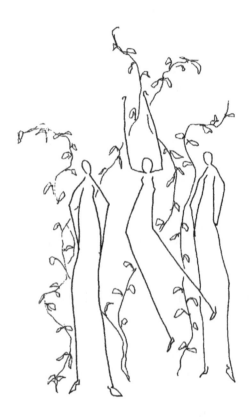

Fill yourself with elements of nature.

Conscious Interface

The drinking in of the dawn's first light is a powerful alchemical process. We invite you to be aware, and fill yourself with other elements of nature.

On a clear night, fill yourself with stars. Allow the vibrations and the natural energy to fill your systems.

Most people are unconscious of what they are allowing to fill their system. When you are unconscious or unaware of the energy vibrations that are permeating your field, you are at the effect.

Be aware of the discordant energies that surround you.

With intention, invite, allow, and welcome the energy of the new day — the energy of the earth under your feet, the trees, the flowers, the oceans, or even colors.

You are working with powerful alchemical processes of healing and restoring. It is a process we call interface — conscious interface.

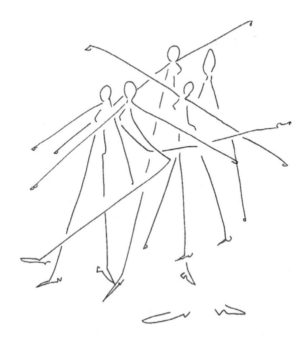

See if you can grab some...

Time

Time responds to your attitude—beliefs, statements, words, and vibrations. Time is one of the fabrics of your earthly game. It is a veil; it keeps you in the illusion.

There is freedom when you shift your beliefs about time. We invite you to be aware of the ways you hold 'time' and your beliefs of 'time'.

When you transform your time beliefs, it is reflected in your physical reality and beyond.

We invite you to play with time... stretch it... mold it... see if you can grab some... step out of time... step into time.

Be gentle with yourself.

Remember to breathe when under time pressure, and remind yourself there is ample time. Remember the importance of laughter.

Practice laughing at time. Take time to laugh. Fill your time with laughter.

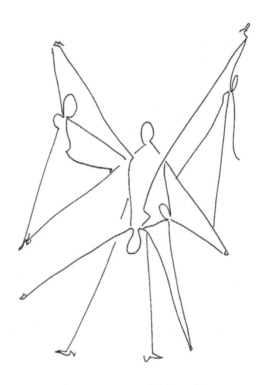

Each moment is always an emotional choice...

Shift Your Focus

You are in the ocean of vibrations of mass consciousness, thought forms and emotional residue. Your vibrations are like a magnet—they will match or attract similar emotions.

Be mindful of your feelings, they will call forth the same from your reality.

Depressions, despair, fear, guilt and worry are dense, slow frequencies.

Each moment is always an emotional choice; strive for the frequency that is higher. Shift your focus; shift your focus; and again, shift your focus.

Gratitude and laughter will shift your frequency. You are a spiritual warrior.

Each moment is your opportunity to transmute any aspect of the denseness, using your conscious heart energy, your breath, your gratitude, your joy, and your love.

It is these frequencies that will lift you up and transmute all else.

Focus on the current step, the current task.

Portal of Now

Practice bringing your awareness into the present NOW and present focus. It is one thing to have this as a concept in the mind, and it is another thing to practice it moment to moment.

Imagine the skill needed to walk a tightrope; each step is in the NOW. If the walker allows themselves to think about the steps beyond the current one, they lose their focus and they lose their balance.

It is by staying in the now, all energy focused on the current step, the task in the moment, that they complete the walk successfully.

Being present in each moment, you are more available to the experience, to others and to yourself.

Notice your breath; notice the space you occupy in the room and in the NOW.

Your portal of power is the NOW.

Recognize your expanded self.

Visual Tunnel

We invite you to recognize your expanded self. Hold your cupped hands to your eye, creating a visual tunnel. What you see in this small window is what you are focusing on in the moment; however, when you remove your hands, an entire vista is available.

Your physical life is the cupped hand version of who you think you are; the expanded vision is who you truly are as a multidimensional being.

Notice when you are looking at your life, a situation or problem with your hands cupped, seeing only the small focused area; take a breath, relax and see the entire vista of possibilities from a larger, more expanded knowing.

We invite you to stay in the present, fully connected to your expanded self in your joy, gratitude, and appreciation.

Maintain emotional balance.

Emotional Waves

You are a complex system of chemicals, hormones, and vibrational frequencies as well as your beliefs, programs, emotional patterns and emotional habits.

It is essential to maintain emotional balance and harmony. Think of it this way: your emotions are like the ebb and flow of the sea.

The sea is affected by the winds, the pull of the moon, the season. It is important to realize that you can either be in the sea of emotions, or be riding the sea of emotions.

Awareness is the boat that allows you to ride your emotional waves. Remember that you are the boat and not the sea.

Ride your emotions, observe your emotions, and allow them to ebb and flow.

If your emotions dump you in the sea, remember — get back in the boat.

Notice who activates you...

Tuning Forks

*E*ach relationship is uniquely different; as your personal vibrations go forth, they are mirrored in the other. Each relationship offers gifts and lessons.

Your vibrations or frequency patterns are the result of experiences, emotional memories, thoughts and beliefs. They are like a tuning fork sending forth a frequency which causes another tuning fork to vibrate in a similar emotional tone. This is entrainment.

Relationships are much like tuning forks in the sense that each human is a series and collection of frequencies and vibrations.

Any discordant frequencies in your personal energy field will call forth matching discordant frequencies or vibrations in the other.

Simply observe who triggers the discordant energies within you; notice who activates your anger or fear. They are your greatest mentors and teachers.

Go to your heart, breathe deeply, blessing them and yourself.

Look for the gift.

Authentic Magnificence

When you resolve the discordant energy you carry, whether it is fear, insecurity, or disapproval, there will be wholeness and healing at your deepest level, thus revealing your most authentic self.

Your quest is to collect the fragments of your divine self, which you have given to past experiences, and bring them home to be healed, integrated and embraced.

In a quiet space, imagine yourself going back to a time in your past; see yourself collecting any energy that you may have left in the form of regret, guilt or incompletion.

Place these energies, memories or experiences in your sacred heart and lovingly offer them for transformation.

Look for the gift. Look for the healing and wholeness that is being called forth by your authentic, magnificent self.

Radiate your approval...

Inner Work

Everything is a vibration. Your interaction with others begins within.

Create a visualization in which you see your loved one bathed in the radiance of your approval, your acceptance, your appreciation, joy and love.

Bathe yourself as well in these vibrations of acceptance, acknowledgement, gratitude, appreciation, joy and love.

Your inner work of acknowledging and empowering others will radiate in your energy field, and will be a vibration that your loved ones will sense and can claim.

You can watch the transformation and healing that will take place. This is true for all relationships.

This inner work will offer you and your loved ones healing. This work also offers healing for the global family.

This is what you are being encouraged to do. This is service work.

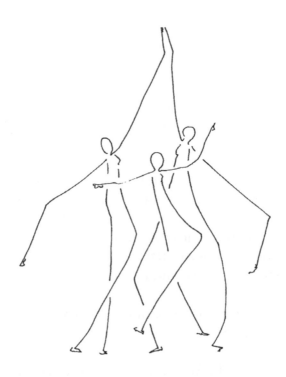

Notice what gets activated...

What Is My Truth?

All relationships are a magnificent way to recognize and integrate every aspect of yourself.

It is the interfacing and the interacting that gives you the opportunity to be fully present, or to be on automatic.

Your automatic responses are like learned dance steps, or a learned script, holding you in a limiting pattern.

Observe yourself in all your relationships. Notice what gets activated; what insecurities, what defensive behaviors or posturing is reflected.

The ego automatically pulls from the past to defend or attack. Relationships can get stuck in these automatic response loops.

Remember each moment you can choose a response that is fresh and new. Ask yourself, "What is my truth in this moment? What would I like to share with this person, this child, this mate, this stranger, that is beyond my standard automatic response?"

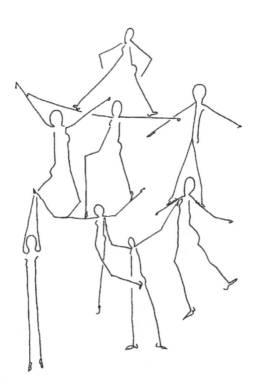

...investigate your reactions.

Be the Detective

Begin to notice how often you are not present in your relationships.

Each person is your mirror, offering you a reflection of some aspect of yourself.

If the reflection is one of pleasure and makes you feel joy, acknowledge that and seek those reflections more often.

If the reflection is one of discomfort and distress, or if the reflection invokes a sense of insecurity, anger, fear, rejection or judgment, then you have a clue to some of your own personal, unresolved issues and automatic projections.

The discovery and awareness of what triggers your issues is a major step in your evolution. Once these unresolved issues and projections are discovered and acknowledged, you can consciously shift them.

Be the detective, investigate your reactions. Be kind and playful in your search. This is a game... lighten up.

Feed your soul and vital life force.

Emotional Buffet

Imagine you are at the emotional buffet table and have a plate in hand.

Life offers you an experience which you can perceive as rejection, and this triggers your anger and sadness. On your plate you have a helping of rejection, some anger and a side of sadness. These are the energetic foods, the emotional vibrations that you are feeding yourself.

Now, imagine a buffet where you serve yourself a helping of joy, spiced with laughter, a huge serving of love and a side of grace. Imagine how delightful that meal would be.

These are high, pure energetic foods that sustain your aliveness; they feed your soul and your vital life force. They add years to your life, assisting your body in rebuilding healthy cells, tissues and bones.

Lovingly feed yourself delicious emotions.

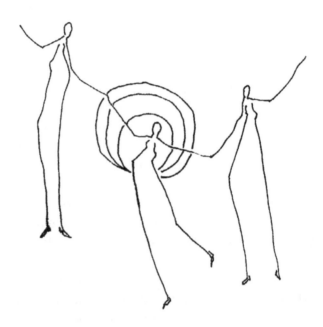

Be open to receive...

Celestial Support

The celestial realms are supporting the transformation of consciousness and awareness that each human is multidimensional.

We invite you to surrender into trust and to consciously ask for any assistance you might need.

Allow your consciousness to expand to the possibility that there is a doorway open to other dimensions, and you have a personal invitation to experience these realms.

State your intentions clearly and surrender; be open to receive the gifts and support. These loving teams of celestial beings are ready to assist and guide you.

When vibrating a cohesive frequency generated by pure emotions, you are more receptive to our support, connection and guidance. Along with maintaining these emotions, it is important to care for the physical body.

Remember to give yourself good nourishment—drink water, allow quiet rest, take deep breaths, and have time outdoors.

Feel or sense a different emotion...

Energetic Patterns

People play out their dysfunctions together through unspoken agreements. Everyone has the power to eliminate these energetic patterns.

Your action in each 'NOW' triggers others, in their magnificence or their own dysfunction. Remember we are all one.

Regret and guilt are toxic emotional energies that hold you in a locked pattern or position.

Visualize a past experience contaminated with your guilt or regret. Create a new result. Imagine acting or speaking differently, being more loving and conscious. Feel or sense a different emotion, one of peace or gratitude. Use this exercise until the past experience has lost its charge.

Do your work. Take action here.

Be strong in your resolve to eliminate dysfunctional patterns. They are sticky, low frequency emotions.

Continue to return to the pure, clear frequencies of joy, gratitude and appreciation.

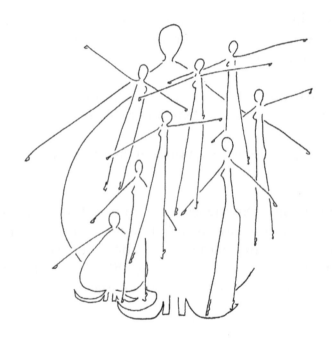

Sense if the foods were prepared lovingly...

Energy Field of Foods

Everything and everyone touches you with their energetic signature; begin to notice this matrix or energy field.

Your goal is to recognize and monitor the frequencies coming in... so that you can and do operate at the smoothest, most optimal and highest vibrations possible.

Notice and place your attention on the energies and tones of all your foods and how these foods affect your body.

Ask yourself, "Does this food create stress in my body or does it add to my over all harmony and wholeness? Does the food have a chaotic, loud energy or a subtle pleasing frequency?"

Be conscious of the vibrations, tones, and frequencies placed there by those who prepare your foods.

You will begin to sense whether the foods were prepared lovingly, or with anger, or frustration, or even in an uncaring, unconscious manner.

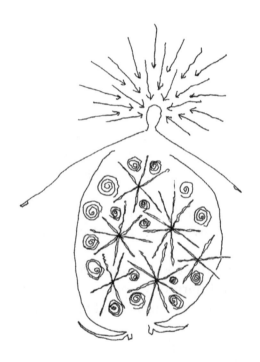

Be mindful of foods you ingest.

Sugar Matrix

We will speak of refined sugar as an energy matrix. Sugar will imbalance and alter your vibrational field; it comes as a jolt to the body and the systems that must process it.

Refined sugar is an accepted, addictive substance on your planet. It is a toxic drug; the body was not designed to process this discordant vibrational frequency on a daily basis.

Sugar places stress on all systems. It creates a type of chaos in the energy field: the body goes into alert and will malfunction over time.

Natural sugar created from honey bees or from fruit has a gentler tone of wholeness.

As your personal energy field becomes more sensitive to all energies, be mindful of the foods you ingest. Be willing to eliminate those that do not serve you.

Review your relationship with sugar and embrace the sweetness of life.

Bless everyone and everything...

A Transformer

You are invited to own your true power, the power that influences the energy matrices of your daily life.

As a multidimensional being, you are a transformer of dense energy vibrations and frequencies.

You always contribute to the energy of your surroundings.

When you place your awareness in your heart and begin to radiate joy or gratitude, your energy field ripples outward into the collective energy matrix. A subtle shift can occur anywhere — at the airport, the shopping mall or a business meeting.

When you are standing in line at the bank, imagine calling in the celestial teams to assist you in energetically cleaning the negative vibrations from the money — stating the intention that all currency is now going out blessing everyone and everything it touches.

This is service work.

Allow yourself to play dress up...

Emotional Garments

We invite you to consider your emotions as garments that you wear. Imagine these garments made of a special fabric that you, your parents, and society have woven from threads of fear, anger, unworthiness, sadness, judgment, unexpressed joy, or withheld love.

When you dress for the day, what emotional garment do you select? Is it an old, comfortable favorite, or is it a new emotional style, woven from emotions that are fresh, alive and in the moment?

Become your own stylist... design some new emotional clothes, try them on, wear them for awhile.

Remember this is just a game. Play! Allow yourself to play dress up... try on different costumes... try on different emotions.

You are invited to clean out your emotional closets.

The emotions that no longer fit can transform to new emotions of gratitude, peace and forgiveness.

Heal any long held grief, sadness or distrust...

Sacred Heart

It is the intelligence of the heart that offers humanity total healing and total connection with the dimensions and the stars.

You are invited to release, transform, and heal any long held grief, sadness or distrust that is carried in your heart.

It is within the sacred heart that the alchemical process of transformation takes place.

If the heart is energetically congested with old emotions of grief or regrets, then the heart is energetically closed to others, and therefore it is closed to the divine.

It is time that humanity heals the wounded heart.

Your life will reflect this healing when your heart is clear and receptive to the divine connection.

Practice radiating love and appreciation from your heart into every moment, every day, offering these coherent emotions into the weaving of this planet's matrix.

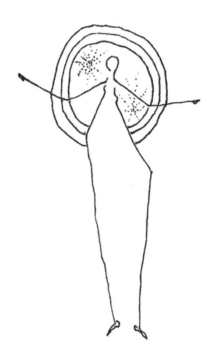

Practice asking your heart...

Your Way Home

We support and encourage you to energetically and emotionally clean out your heart space. Polish it, shine it up, air it out and begin to live there with joy.

It is the heart's knowing that will guide and uplift you in all your actions.

Practice asking your heart before you ask your mind.

Practice bridging and connecting the heart's intelligence with the brain's intelligence.

Practice radiating unconditional love, joy, gratitude and appreciation from the heart.

Allow yourself consciously to dwell within your sacred heart space as often as possible.

Allow yourself to see your sacred heart space as spacious, infinite, expanded and whole. It is your link to the cosmic grid. It is your connection to the global matrix. It is your way home.

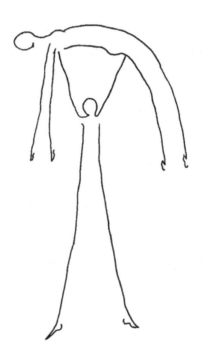

Play life with relish...

"Lighten" Up

We invite you to play a game. When an old emotion of "not enough" time or money comes into your consciousness, stop what you are doing and follow the thread of the thought. Trace it back as far as possible, release it, and replace it with your heart's desire.

Make a conscious decision to shift, release, and transform whatever the emotion, thought, memory or belief that is pulling you down.

In this hologame, when one individual uplifts, heals or transforms some aspect of their personal shadow or limitation, they shift the entire matrix.

We invite you to "lighten" up. Be in your joy. Play life with relish and passion.

It is from joy, gratitude and appreciation that all things flow. Know you are loved and supported always; call upon this knowing.

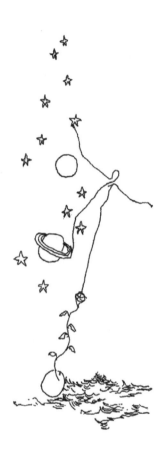

Work in tandem with spirit...

Listen to the Stars

Reality seems limited to what you can see, feel or touch; these limitations act as a blindfold to your extra sensory remembering.

The universe is a complex matrix where parallel realities exist. Portals of energy can be activated or closed, and traveling dimensions is merely a shift of one's consciousness, frequency, or vibration.

Your planet is surrounded by multiple energy grids. The ability to sense these grids, to work in tandem with spirit and the stars to maintain, repair, and activate these coordinates is the work of all multidimensional starhumans.

Portals, matrices, energy grids, power places, star travel, and dimensional shifts are all juicy places to focus and cultivate into your daily life.

Other dimensions are as close as your breath. Stars communicate with every cell.

You are invited to listen to the stars, and sense the other realms and dimensions.

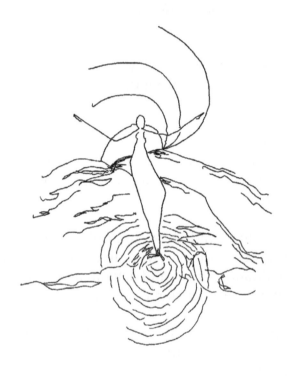

Ride the wave of a blessed flow...

The Zone

As a multidimensional being, in your personal power, you are capable of consciously gifting a greater and purer vibration into any energy field you choose.

In this state of awareness you are riding the wave of a blessed flow. With no resistance, no pushing against, there is just synergy, a movement of events and delicious happenings—some call this the "zone". We call this being fully present to your divine magnificence.

Stay conscious in all activities.

Be aware that you can add a pure vibration of uplifting clarity, gratitude and appreciation while standing in line at the store. Others will feel this frequency which allows a shift.

This energy work is a service and can be done while you are present in the space, or from a distance while in the privacy of your mediations or prayers.

Sing, dance, and praise.

Refocus on JOY

Today, focus on what is right in your life. Remove your attention from your worries. Put your worries in a basket. You can keep the basket within sight, just be aware when you are tempted to fondle or caress any worry.

Take this moment, this hour, this day, and be grateful for what is working in your life.

Stay conscious of the smallest, simplest blessings and always acknowledge them.

When a worry thought surfaces, stop in the very moment of its creation and refocus; express your joy and gratitude. Nothing is more important today than making this emotional and mental shift.

Practice offering appreciation for everything and everyone.

Bathe your entire experience in your joy and playfulness. Sing, dance, and praise.

Give this day your joy—clear, strong, colorful, and out loud. Be in your joy. Be joy!!!

Heal your discordant emotions.

Blueprint of Perfection

It is your divine right and power as a multidimensional being in a human form, to transform and heal your discordant emotions and painful experiences. This healing will affect the entire matrix.

Look at the pain your parents carried; with understanding, love them free. You are doing this work for your own healing, no matter what the abuse, pain, or the rejection; with conscious willingness, offer these emotions to the light of transformation.

You can use laughter, sounds, singing, prayers, intentions, and forgiveness; these are just a few methods that are available to shift these old, dense painful experiences.

We see you as perfect and invite you to allow that blueprint of perfection to infuse your physical form. We honor and support you.

You are the transformers. You are the light bearers. You are magnificent star beings.

Lift your thoughts, feelings and words...

Conscious Flying

When you are in the energy field of doubting and negative thoughts, it is like walking.

You are invited to fly, to lift thoughts, feelings and words into the higher realms of conscious energy, the realms of unlimited possibilities.

You know the power of intent—the power of your vibrations of joy, gratitude, appreciation, and the grace of allowing your desires to manifest.

You have given your conscious attitude wings. You have learned to fly—vibration by vibration, thought by thought, word by word.

When you are around those who fly, it is easier to practice flying. When you are around walkers, who don't know they can fly, it can trigger doubts and limitations, so you begin to walk rather than fly.

We invite you to go to the edge, jump off and practice flying.

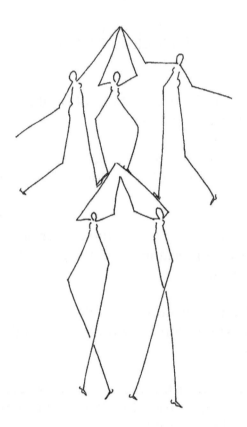

Transform your doubts...

Laser Beam of Gratitude

When you hold your vision in your purest frequency of allowing and receiving, it invites the highest and purest desires to manifest.

We invite you to stay in your joy. When struggle or difficulty pops up, see yourself sending a focused laser beam of gratitude to the doubts.

Keep this process juicy. Keep this process exciting. Keep this process delicious.

This is an opportunity for you to truly practice knowing and creating from the heart. The energy will align behind you and open doors that were invisible before this moment.

Laugh and delight in the process while you are transforming your own doubts as well as the doubts and confusion in the matrix.

As a multidimensional star being, you know a far bigger reality.

Allow your dreams to be big, bright, and clear.

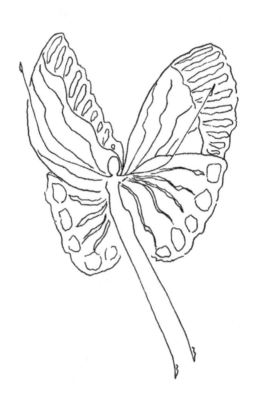

Ride the energy...

Welcome Change

Welcome change. Embrace change. Through change all things grow, regenerate, transmute, transform, metamorphose, and reorganize.

Find joy in the opportunity that is offered by change. Find your gratitude for what the new experience is gifting. Discover what you can appreciate in the changing of plans.

Your reality is not fixed or solid or static. It is ever evolving and shifting. Think of the chrysalis just before it emerges as the beautiful butterfly.

Change always offers the invitation for transformation in some form.

You are emerging from your chrysalis, stretching your multidimensional wings. Welcome the opportunity. Ride the energy of change in a graceful smooth manner, like the butterfly.

Your coherent emotions of joy, gratitude, and appreciation held in your sacred heart are your wings during these times of change.

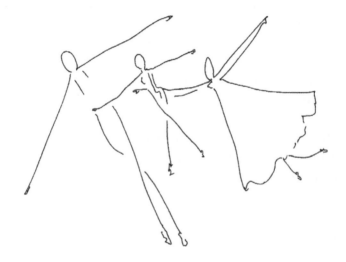

Move into the flow like the hawk soaring.

The Wind Stream

Observe hawks that soar; they move into the flow of the wind stream and are carried aloft with only a slight feather movement.

It appears to be a miracle, and a miracle is a supernatural phenomenon. When the hawk soars effortlessly on the wind stream, he does not consider it a miracle, he considers it wisdom. He knows he is one with the flow of energy and he rides it.

The wind stream is created by the vibrations that are being offered to the matrix.

By maintaining a frequency of joy, gratitude, and appreciation you can move through your day effortlessly, like the hawk soaring.

The ultimate aim for the awakened starhuman is the knowledge that they are one with the divine flow or wind stream in which all things expand with ease and grace.

Allow the universe to support your life.

Miracles Are the Rule

You either struggle or flow in your life. It is that simple.

When you find yourself struggling with anything, stop and reset the vibrations you are sending to the field.

Become a conscious monitor of your thoughts, feelings and projections. When you radiate the clear vibration of a higher frequency, you allow the incredible workings of the universe to support your life.

You are one with the field of all possibilities.

You become one with the results. Your life becomes awesome. You inspire others to lift their consciousness.

You step into a space in which miracles and synchronicity are the rule. In this space, a clear intention will manifest the quickest and easiest way possible.

The consciousness of the energy field delights in bringing you results in wondrous and grace-filled ways.

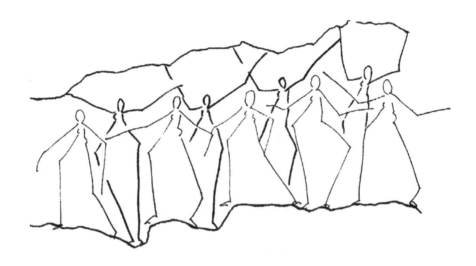

You see what you believe.

Think Outside the Box

Begin to stretch your beliefs, stretch your knowing. Think outside the box.

Notice when you feel limited, your thoughts don't empower, you feel shut down or trapped. When this happens, you are touching the sides of your limitation box.

Notice when you sense there is something more that could unfold.

In these moments when you can shift your frequency, you also shift your mental vibration and begin to allow another reality to emerge.

Practice stretching, expanding your viewpoint and perception. This practice allows the sides of your belief box to expand to include something that you would "normally" consider impossible or unreal.

Wondrous possibilities are always available. Remember, you see what you believe.

Joy, gratitude, and appreciation allows you to "disappear" your box of limited thinking, to remember your multidimensional starself.

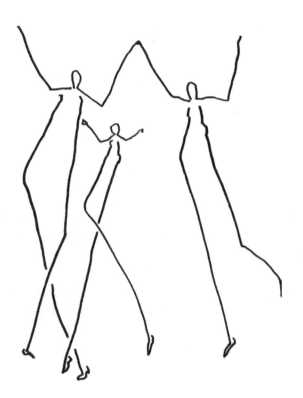

Monthly Morning Messages Transmissions

We Welcome Your Partnership...
—July 2008

We embrace you, knowing the changes that your life is undergoing. You are riding the wave of this exciting awaking. You are the conscious ones showing the way to those around you.

Know that your intentions and your energy truly make a difference. Step into this knowing and this service.

Call upon the celestial beings, for support, inspiration and assistance with your physical journey.

We invite your partnership. We welcome your partnership. Be at peace, beloved.

Rapid Change...
— August 2008

The changes that are occurring are happening in rapid succession.

The first reaction to change is to tense up and resist, to even drop into a frequency of fear and worry.

The best way to ride the rapids of these changes is to surrender... relax into trust, take deep breaths often, stay in your heart awareness, stay in your gratitude and welcome the LIGHT!

This is why you are here, to transform and transmute any limiting dysfunctional energy by holding a coherent frequency of harmony and peace.

We are here to support and honor you as this evolution and these tremendous changes take place.

Anchor the Vision...

—September 2008

We say to each of you, beloved ones, continue to bless all that is before you. Step into your personal power knowing that you are "Transformers" of the dense dysfunctional energy that you are witnessing.

It is by your clear intent and coherent emotions offered into the collective matrix and field, that a true shift will take place.

Radiate your conscious and dedicated feelings from your heart as a soothing and transforming elixir to all suffering.

Hold the vision of the reality you want to embrace and support. Anchor this vision into the collective, the quantum energy field, and call it forward.

We are here to support and honor you as this evolution and these tremendous changes take place.

Transformation Happens...
—October 2008

We are here. We honor and acknowledge your personal magnificence. We invite you to clearly own your power to make a difference.

We invite each of you to return to a centered, balanced place as often as necessary in order to hold a vision and anchor that vision into your dimension.

It is the collective, awake, aware and conscious beings that are the most powerful force available. When you send out a beam of your light, when you send forth a wave of gratitude and appreciation from your heart, transformation happens.

The more magnificent, multidimensional star beings that practice conscious heart service, the greater the impact is for change. This is your gift.

We say again, you are powerful beyond measure; claim your power.

You can offer a coherent frequency of joy, gratitude and appreciation at any time and any place you find yourself. These coherent vibrations join other like vibrations and become the trim tab that stabilizes the rocking of the collective boat.

Call upon the celestial beings for assistance and partnership.

When you continue to consciously shift and return to a state of gratitude and compassion, you are receptive to guidance as well as right action.

Renew from Within...

— December 2008

We invite you to dedicate this time to renew from within, to acknowledge your divineness and the divineness of others.

It is a time to honor yourself by stretching beyond your personal fears of any limitations.

Hold firm to the awareness of your magnificence as co-creator of your reality. It is important to hold a pure, coherent frequency — to be the energetic tone of clarity and truth, as the outer world undergoes a transformation, a shift of the ages.

When there is chaos, fear, turmoil and confusion, there is a call for awake beings of light to step forward in their strength and anchor that light in the matrix.

You can choose to vibrate with the chaos, fear, turmoil and confusion — or vibrate clarity, gratitude, compassion and joy.

Remember WHO YOU ARE, and know without a doubt that you are MASTERS, magnificent, multidimensional beings.

This is the time for you to shine the truth and offer this truth to all. Know that you are blessed, and be at peace, beloveds.

Light of Transmutation...
— February 2009

There are those who are feeling pushed up against the wall of their imagined limitations.

They are experiencing the time shift as the collective moves through this evolutional stage. There are many old patterns and paradigms that are being uprooted and transformed.

Each individual is being invited to step out of their personal and the collective fear, and embrace these tremendous changes. This is the opportunity you came here to transform.

Remember that you are magnificent, multidimensional Star souls. You are powerful beyond measure. You are transformers of dense dysfunctional energy.

Smile, and even laugh at your fears; give your fears and concerns to the Light of Transmutation.

Be willing to allow and expect incredible miracles to occur in your life and affairs, even when your seeming reality is falling apart.

Remember to hold a pure, coherent emotion within your heart portal of love, compassion, gratitude and appreciation. This action on your part will support and assist the best and the brightest results.

Request the presence of the Divine Forces, and together radiate the vision of the highest and most joyous manifestation for all. Remember all is well and more.

See a Better Future...

—March 2009

Allow a brighter future to pull you forward. In the midst of this upheaval in the collective reality, each individual has their story which reflects their personal challenges.

It is the personal challenges that are yours to transform.

There are always many ways to look at a current problem. We invite you to look at any personal issue from the most expanded place as possible.

Find some blessing, some opportunity, something to be grateful for in the situation you find yourself. Spend time throughout the day envisioning a new result, a brighter outcome.

Remember that you are masters, multidimensional masters, at creating realities; step into your true power.

Begin to see a better future; hold your vision with passion and clarity. Energetically wrap yourself in this possible future, feel it, sense it, and allow it to feel as real as possible. Allow this future to pull you forward.

Allow the energy field of all possibilities to become your partner—know that your thoughts, words and feelings are always interacting with this field of energy. Be mindful of the quality of messages that you are sending into this receptive quantum field.

Practice asking for the best; practice allowing and receiving the awesome potential outcomes.

Remember to ask for assistance from the realms of Light and Love.

Your Blessings Will Uplift...

— April 2009

I wanted to share the personal message I received from the "team" about both of my loved ones. I believe this message is one to be shared with everyone as we experience the challenges of the changes in our lives and in the lives of our family and friends.

It is important to remember that it is far more effective to hold all that you are concerned with in the container of gratitude. It may seem difficult, however, we invite you to continue to be creative and envision the best, rather than worry about the worst.

Begin to see the most amazing outcome happening and hold that vision with the tenderness of a gardener for her new seedling. You are far more effective in supporting their healing and well-being by seeing them at their best. When a thought of concern or worry comes to your active mind, quickly find something about this situation in which you are grateful. It can be a simple gratitude. Pre-plan these gratitudes, have a file of miracles — blessings easily ready to grab when needed.

The minute you are aware that you are dropping into a place of worry or concern, take a deep breath, sigh and replace the worry thought with one that has a lighter flavor, a more coherent frequency. This is a conscious exercise, it is what is yours to do right now. You can be the anchor for your loved ones to hold on to, the vibration that they will entrain with, the link to their strength and well-being.

During these times of great change and great evolutionary shifts, it is most important for those who are aware to hold a firm and stable platform for all those who are striving to transform some dysfunction.

Remember that you are a transformer; everyone is a transformer of dense, dysfunctional patterns and energy.

However these dysfunctional patterns and energy manifest in your life and the lives of others, they are there to be processed and transformed through the conscious system of an awakened multidimensional being. This is the same tool to use with any situation and thought patterns that do not support your joy and well-being—whether it is health, finances, personal relationships, jobs or family.

You can align yourself with the flow of well-being and joy simply by holding a clear and firm frequency of gratitude. The mind loves to solve problems, to worry, to fret, to be concerned. That is what the mind loves to do, and the mind will hijack your time doing just that. This is the old paradigm; this is what you are shifting and transforming. Realize that it is just a pattern of thought; it is just an old emotional frequency that still resides inside the system of your mind. It is important to understand and realize that you are moving into a new paradigm in which you will hold a vision, a thought, and intention of what you desire to manifest and it will be so.

So this day we invite you to return to a state of gratitude as often and as frequently as possible.

Know that your loved ones also have patterns to shift and transform, that is theirs to do. Know that your loved ones are also magnificent, multidimensional beings who agreed to assist in the transformation of dysfunction on this planet, in all its many forms. Each one has a purpose, an assignment, a soul agreement that they are in the process of completing. Support them with your highest and best thoughts and emotions for them. They will feel this on the subtle planes of consciousness. Your blessings will embrace them and lift them up; your joy will light their way.

We invite you to call upon the celestial and divine realms of truth, love and light; assistance and support is as close as your request. Know that we are always as near as your heartbeat and as close as your breath. Be at peace beloved, know that all is well.

Humans of Light...
—May 2009

We greet you and acknowledge your radiance. We invite you to express yourself as the true beings of light that you are. You are homo-luminous, humans of light. It is time for each person to recognize and honor this powerful aspect of themselves.

During these times of great upheaval and changes that are taking place on the screen of reality, it is your gift of light that will support the shift in others. We speak of the light that is transforming the landscapes of your consciousness.

More and more individuals are "waking up" to the awareness that they are magnificent, multidimensional transformers of dense, dysfunctional energy.

Each time you personally recognize a thought pattern or behavior that is limiting or judgmental, and you make a conscious shift to a thought that is softer, more open, more accepting... you can consider that "moment of mental/ emotional shifting" a packet of light.

It now becomes a "de-light-filled", conscious game to realize that these mental/emotional vibrations carry energy, energy that you are personally responsible to transform.

Each time you shift or transform a thought that is dense with fear or worry, you add LIGHT to the matrix and the collective consciousness of humanity. YOU BECOME THE TRANSFORMER, thought-by-thought, emotion-by-emotion, moment-by-moment, and day-by-day. Each day, your radiance increases.

We acknowledge each of you for the personal work that you are doing to uplift your reality by your own awakening of behaviors, patterns, thought and emotions that hold vibrations of denseness and dysfunction.

When you choose to express your best and highest self, you begin to embody the light.

This light energy gradually shifts the physical circuits, your nervous systems, the neo-pathways and your very cells. Your body carries more and more of a light frequency, more and more coherent energy that radiates as light. You become a being of light.

We see you as beautiful, luminous beings becoming brighter. Be at peace and know that all is well and more.

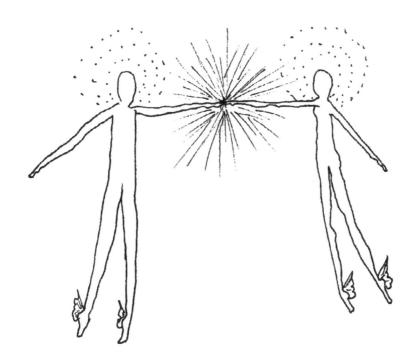

Self Care...

—June 2009

Beloveds, we greet you with our open-hearted gratitude for the incredible forces of light that you are creating. Your impact on the collective is being felt. Your radiance continues to expand, especially as you recognize the true nature of who you are as a multidimensional being—realizing that you are not your physical body; you are celestial in nature and size.

You are conscious that your energy field is directed by your thoughts and emotions, focused through your heart. We acknowledge the incredible expansion that is being offered to the collective. We honor you for this service.

However, it is most important that we remind you that during the tumultuous times, the times of great change on your planet, that you take care of your personal vehicle, your physical body. Self care of your human aspect is most important.

You are awakening to the awareness of your sensitivity to the distress and the pain expressed in the collective. Assisting in the transformation of this distress and pain is an aspect of service you are all stepping forward to do.

Yet, self care must come first, taking care of the physical body by proper foods, good water, rest and time spent in nature are keys to the well-being of all homo-luminous beings. Be mindful of your sugar intake—white processed sugar will imbalance and alter your vibrational field.

There are many energy tools and methods available to keep your personal energy domain clear. Be responsible to practice energy hygiene. Use intention, visualizations, sounds, laughter, chants and movements to clear stuck energy immediately. Imagine taking an energy shower which will clear the frequency of others from your field.

Imagine using colors streaming through your body. Imagine bathing in colored pools of healing water. Create a sacred healing space in the celestial realms; imagine yourself in this space being restored to your own divine integrity.

Make the intention of disconnecting or unplugging any energy cords or attachments that do not belong to you; send back any emotions or thought forms that are not yours. Be sure to send them back to where they belong, blessed and transformed.

After you have cleared the attachments, the thought forms, and the emotions that do not belong to you, be sure to always invite your own divine essence to completely fill you.

We invite you to begin to practice these energy clearings often during your day. When you are overwhelmed with emotion of fear, scarcity, and depression, ask yourself what percent of this is mine and what percent is the collectives. This gives you a perspective.

Become aware of shielding your personal energy field; practice using the inter-dimensional tool, the *Holon, which sets up a field of protection around your body.

Be mindful of your thoughts and words. You are the vanguard, the forefront, and the sentinels of light in this exquisite expansion of consciousness and evolution.

We invite you to take care of yourself first, and then offer your clear, balanced power to others. We again offer you our gratitude as well as our assistance for the service that you contribute in all aspects of your journey.

Remember, all is well—be at peace.

*Holon of Protection, www.tomkenyon.com

Galactic Portal...

—July 2009

We are here. It is our delight to connect with you in this manner. It is important for you to have this information so that you may utilize this energy to the highest and the best for yourself and your planet.

You are experiencing a galactic portal. There are others offering information, support and awareness to humanity and this hologame during this intense influx of energy. The celestial brethren are offering your beloved planet a powerful download of consciousness and potentiality.

This force has been building, and the lunar eclipse of the full moon* opened the door fully. This energy is offering the opportunity to transform any limitations. While you are experiencing these next few weeks, be mindful to use this powerful download to the maximum, allowing yourself to be recalibrated.

This is an opportunity to bring balance and healing of the masculine and the feminine energies in all aspects of your planet and within your own field. This is a gift of the highest degree. You are being invited to be the chalice for this energy as it is anchored within your matrix of consciousness, and therefore the global matrix of mass consciousness.

Look within—gift yourself the permission, the grace and forgiveness to truly step into your stellar magnificence. What would that look like in your life; what would shift or change?

Utilize this energy that is being given during this galactic portal to assist you in healing what is ready to be healed and released. Look within and welcome the balance of your own masculine and feminine aspects.

Ask for celestial assistance, use consciousness tools; visualize and dream a better world for yourself and the planet. Step into this power; allow it to bath you; and allow this illumination to activate codes in your personal matrix. This energy is offering you the opportunity to step fully into your radiance as a being of light, and the awareness of your multidimensionality.

The period of time that this galactic gateway is open will continue to increase in intensity. Allow yourself to ride this incredible wave; embrace this extraordinary vibration of change and transformation.

Remember to take care of yourself — rest, eat well, drink water and be in nature. Notice any changing sleep patterns and body sensations that are uncomfortable; remember to breathe into any uncomfortable sensations or thoughts.

Toss all doubts that come up of your success, well-being and abundance into this energy for transmutation.

Return often to feelings of joy, gratitude and appreciation. These frequencies will support and assist you to maintain balance. Ask for divine support and assistance. Be kind to yourself and others. You are surfing the big one right now.

Your gifts to humanity are your conscious willingness and the chalice of your sacred heart portal which anchors this divine transmission. This is evolution.

Be embraced by our gratitude, deep love and respect for this service you are offering to humanity. Be at peace and know that all is well and more.

July 7, 2009 was a Full Moon Lunar Eclipse, July 21/22, 2009 Solar Eclipse, and August 5, 2009 is the last Lunar Eclipse of this gateway. Note — Every eclipse offers an opportunity and energy exchange for humanity.

Activate Your Mastery...

— August 2009

We greet you with our gratitude for the work and service you are offering to the collective grid. Each individual is facing incredible challenges in their personal lives, as well as observing the incredible challenges that are taking place on the screen of reality.

We remind you, dear ones, that you are truly the magnificent transformers of all that is before you, in your personal lives and your connections to the collective events that are unfolding.

We realize that the energy that has been bathing each of you during these last celestial offerings has added a level of stress. Many are experiencing changes in sleep patterns, and other disruptions manifesting as imbalances within our body. These disturbance are occurring as you integrate this energetic shift into your systems.

Be aware of any old fears and insecurities that resurface and are triggered. This is where your mastery can be activated; this is your opportunity to shine and illuminate all that is before you. We invite you to use all the energetic tools that you have collected during your own personal evolution.

Recognize and acknowledge your true power to affect the challenging aspects of your life, by holding the clear vision and intention for the most supportive outcome.

We invite you to call on assistance from the celestial realms. When the physical and non-physical realms are together in true partnership, there is an even greater power for transformation.

This is truly your service as a divine, multidimensional beings. Be embraced with our gratitude, love and support.

You Begin to Shine...
—September 2009

We are here! We express our deep gratitude to each of you for claiming your true power to transform the energy matrix surrounding the financial aspects of your planet. This work is just beginning. However, we assure you that each time you do your personal work regarding how you hold the vibrations of your finances and the out picturing of the global financial climate, you are making a significant difference. This is where you begin to shine.

It is by owning your power as a conscious being, stepping into that true power to make a difference. It is the knowledge that you are connected to others of like mind and heart who are also doing this work/service.

We have acknowledged that these are challenging times for each of you. This is why you are here, to transform and uplift the dysfunction of this planet and the dysfunction that is in your personal life. What appears in your life as challenges are truly opportunities to raise your conscious heart energy, and like a laser beam, shine that intention to all that appears discordant. This is the true act of service to humanity.

It is by offering your conscious heart awareness as a healing balm of energy into any situation, that it is uplifted, and it is transformed. YOU ARE TRANSFORMERS! Own that; live that reality; know in your deepest heart that you are here to transform any of the negative, painful, limited experiences.

NO ONE HAS MORE POWER TO TRANSFORM ENERGY THAN YOU! Each human, must step up to this reality, ownership and awareness, and claim their true sovereignty and power. We remind you of your birthright; claim your partnership—call upon the Divine Force, the Celestial Realms, and the Creator Source to support and assist you in all ways, always. The time is now. Your part in this unfolding is valuable, unique, and important. We surround you with our love and gratitude.

Offer Your Highest...
— October 2009

We greet you, beloved transformers—we embrace you with our gratitude and acknowledgment for the clarity of purpose that you are living your life. Each and every individual, magnificent being is being called to offer their highest and their best to the evolution that is taking place in the hearts and minds of humanity.

Each of you is experiencing these energy shifts, these dimensional shifts, in your own unique manner. You are claiming your power to transform the dysfunctions in your lives and in the world around you. These challenges can take on many forms—financial hardships, and health issues, loss of loved ones, homes or jobs.

There is also the confusion, fear and anxiety of the collective consciousness. As you move between the energetic dimensions and levels of awareness, you are each beginning to realize your personal mission.

You are recognizing the places that you can and do make a difference. This difference can be on a physical level of assisting another, or it can be on the energetic level with your intentions, prayers and focus.

More and more magnificent beings are stepping up to the tasks at hand, finding ways to serve that make their hearts sing; the places where their passion and their caring can be offered to the collective. We see this energy field growing daily, as hearts and minds are connecting for the good of all.

We see your shinning energy radiating into the collective consciousness, shinning upon the dysfunctions of your society.

We see your collective mindfulness and simple actions gathering strength, and as this strength builds, it impacts everything and everyone that does not honor the highest and the best for all.

We offer and maintain our support to each of you upon request. Your request can be for assistance at the personal level, or your request can be at the collective level.

Know that we will respond to your call with an embrace of love and guidance. It is our honor to work closely with you. For as you evolve, we evolve. We send you blessings of our respect and honor for who you are as divine celestial beings.

Know that you are loved.

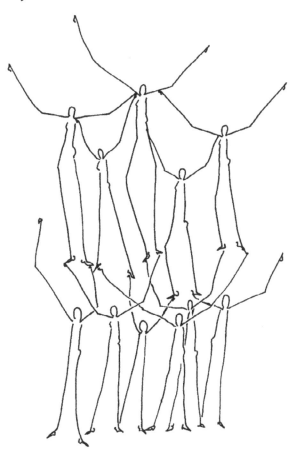

Transforming the Frequency of Fear...

— November 2009

Greetings, beloveds—it is our honor to connect with you through these written words and also in the sacred space of your heart. We will speak to you about fear, and invite you to recognize and own your personal fear.

Fear is the frequency in the collective consciousness that is affecting everyone. Each individual has their own private fears. It is most important as transformers to shift and uplift these personal and private fears. We invite each of you to review where you are fearful. Recognize what triggers your peculiar fears. This is the work that you are being called to transform and shift for yourself and the collective.

Examine the frequency and vibration of fear in your life. Where does fear live in your body? What thoughts are tinged with fear? Is it the fear of loss, of your job, your home, and/or your loved ones? When you allow your fears to effect your thoughts and actions, you are powerless. We know this is not the truth.

You are a magnificent, multidimensional being of light and love. You are a transformer, and you are being asked to step into the energy field of the dysfunctions of fear to uplift the frequency.

Be mindful of the promotion of all fear, whether it is in your news media, your cinema, or communications throughout the internet. Fear is a malignant vibration. It spreads and expands according to the chaos within the system.

Each time you encounter fear, whether it is within your own feelings and thoughts or is being promoted through your media, stop and shift this low, dense vibration and emotion as quickly and as often as possible.

When you are vibrating a high, coherent frequency of love and gratitude, you surround yourself with a protective energy field of grace, which allows you to be guided in the best and safest ways.

These are changing times, and there is an evolution occurring within your very cells. This transmutation is occurring within humanity. It is common for humans to store their emotions in their cells. Therefore, this metamorphosis from the dense low frequency of fear and carbon-based material into the high frequency vibration of love, compassion, joy and gratitude generates and allows each cell to radiate more light.

You are becoming a Light Being. Your mission is to allow and welcome this metamorphosis within.

Each time you choose to release the low, heavy, dense vibration of fear, you allow more energetic light to be present in each cell. Your release work is done with your willingness to recognize your fears and process them consciously. The chaos and challenges will begin to shift as well with this collective transformation.

Every time you embrace your fears and give them a voice of freedom and release, you invite grace-light into your life and you add to the collective evolution. We offer you our love and support; we join you in your sacred heart, where all is healed and transformed.

Remember, you are a transformer of dense energy; you are a magnificent being of consciousness and Light. You are held in the embrace of love.

Step into Your Light...

— December 2009

Greetings beloveds, it is our honor to connect with you through these written words, and also in the sacred space of your heart. We embrace you, each one, with our love and support. We offer you our deepest appreciation for the work that you are doing in your life and in the field of the collective consciousness.

We have observed the tremendous difficulties you have faced in your personal experiences and the challenges that you have been invited to transform. We have seen your courage as you have confronted health issues, loss of loved ones, and the loss of your homes and jobs. We acknowledge your strength as you have continued to embrace all that was before you.

These are the times on your planet in which there is great chaos and upheaval in the systems. These are the times, the times of change when what is unlike the highest and the best for all is being dismantled.

We know, that from your perspective in the physical form, these are times of great uncertainty which create fear and distrust. However, we continue to encourage you to know without doubt, that you are truly a magnificent, multidimensional being of light.

While your physical form has its limitations, you are becoming more and more aware of your divine Self. It is the magnificent, divine aspect that we acknowledge and call forth in you. You are a transformer of dense, dysfunctional energy.

Your heart consciousness and intention for good is more powerful than you allow yourself to realize. We are inviting you to step into that knowing and into that powerful place of transforming all that appears in your reality and in your personal experience.

144

You are being invited to work consciously in the energy fields of all possibilities to transform any discordant energy that arises within your personal matrix, and then expanding that into the collective matrix. This is a moment-to-moment mission and opportunity. You have all the skills and abilities as a master of transformation.

Play full out, step into your LIGHT and step into your POWER. Know without a doubt that you are needed and that your personal work and service is of great value to the whole.

Each time you shift your expression of fear or worry into an emotion of trust and hope, you are doing global service work. Each time you correct the words that you send forth, so that they are nurturing and supportive to others, you are doing global service work.

These are exciting times to hold the vision of the best possible outcome of all that is unfolding. Bless all the world leaders so that they are inspired to act with integrity and for the well-being of all. Remember, the chalice of your heart is your power source of change.

We say to you again, never doubt for a minute how important YOU are to this collective work and service of transformation.

These are the times in which your divine SELF came here to serve, to offer your consciousness as gifts of transmutation and your LIGHT for the benefit of humanity. Wherever you stand in life, begin there. Each action of kindness, each shift of consciousness, and each opportunity to offer healing energy to another or a situation adds to the total uplifting of humankind.

Know that you are seen, acknowledged and supported by the celestial beings of love and light. Know you are loved and greatly appreciated.

Claim Your True Power...

—January 2010

Greetings beloved being of LIGHT, it is our honor to connect with you in this manner. We know that you can feel the energy transmission we offer through these words. Humanity is stepping into a new, ever-expanding phase of evolution; you are stepping into a new reality, a reality that is being called forth from your heart consciousness.

There is a pause occurring in time that many are feeling. This pause is allowing you to adjust to a new frequency. You intuitively sense something is different, yet when you look out into the world things seem the same. That sameness is shifting; there is a tremendous influx of energy that is bathing each of you and your reality.

This new energy has never been felt before, so there is a feeling of puzzlement as well as a deep recognition from that aspect of you that is multidimensional and all knowing. Even though the outer reality seems the same, and the issues this planet is facing still looms ahead of you, there has been a significant shift in the realms of truth and transformation.

We acknowledge each of you for your incredible support. Your clear intentions and heart-felt vibrations have anchored this new wave of transformation and transparency, which is beginning to filter down into physical manifestation for you to observe. This next period of time will seem to morph and stretch in unusual ways.

Do not be surprised by what will unfold as you are straddling multi-dimensions, moving back and forth between the old and the new, adjusting and reestablishing your presence and frequency to match the reality that you have anchored in your dreams and visions. Hold firm to those dreams and visions; allow them a home in your heart and consciousness.

Welcome the upheavals—the changes as they appear in your life, and the unfolding events around the world. Remember that you are the one calling forth this new consciousness of realized and recognized oneness. Hold the anchor for the frequencies coming in order to activate those who continue to slumber or resist their true awareness of oneness.

Celebrate and claim your true power—acknowledge, appreciate and own your ability to make a difference. Honor yourself for the strength and courage you carry in this physical walk in life. Honor yourself for the experiences that you have been willing to transform. Honor yourself as the conscious heart that you are. You chose to do this incredible service for yourself and all mankind, and we embrace you with our gratitude.

Continue to maintain a frequency of grace and gratitude, for these vibrations and frequencies will allow you to surf the tumultuous energy fields that change brings. These are exciting and thrilling times of divine unfolding. Allow yourself to walk in grace through the days ahead, uplifting all that is before you.

Be mindful to care for your physical body as it also experiences the changes of dimensions. Celebrate as often as possible what is right in the world, for this attitude continues to anchor and call forth the true connection and oneness with all.

We celebrate you, we honor you and we surround you with our love and gratitude for the expression of your unique magnificence.

We See You!...

—February 2010

We greet you with our love and appreciation. We embrace you with our gratitude and acknowledgement.

Each of you is anchoring the opportunity of transformation by your very presence in this time frame and dimension. It is important for you to acknowledge your role and place in this incredible evolution. This is not a time to be shy; this is not a time to be fearful; and this is not a time to hesitate. This is a time to truly claim your authority and sovereignty as the divine being that you truly are.

These changes, and this transformation of consciousness that is occurring and continues to expand, are because of your participation. It is a tremendous opportunity as you remember your magnificence, your power and your deep love for humanity. These are the times for which you have been awaiting.

Look in your personal life and see what is up to be transformed and shifted into the light of awareness and truth. What emotions are you still carrying, what regrets or sorrows, what resentments and prejudices? These dense, dysfunctional energies that you, as a human, have experienced — the emotional and physical abuses are yours to personally transform. They are your inherent responsibly. You have a personal invitation to offer these dense energies of pain and suffering up for release. It is your willing intention in your sacred heart chalice that you bring these energies to the light. When you consciously take action, this is divine service. You are a transformer of energy.

Look at the energy blockages in your personal life, your relationships with others, with finances, and with health; and begin to honestly, and with joy, release them. Sound them; pray them; dance them; and move these blockages out of their holding patterns. It is time! Now is the time when you have the most divine and celestial support to do this work for yourself and for the collective. This is your job. Remember as you transform your personal emotional issues, this energy ripples out to the collective and others are uplifted and healed as well. When you do your individual transforming work of forgiveness, and the release of old, dense patterns and dysfunctions, your loved ones are quickened as well.

If you observe heavy, dense energy vibrations of hatred, anger, or conflict, we invite you to immediately offer a higher vibration of compassion, love and forgiveness. You are not powerless. You are absolutely powerful beyond measure. Do not hesitate to step into this active role as a transformer. Your numbers are increasing as more individuals are awakening to this realization that they actively participate and interface with the energy vibrations in the collective. More and more magnificent, multidimensional humans are recognizing that they are influencing the out-picturing of reality. Celebrate this awareness, and join with others in this incredible field of all possibilities.

Hold the vision of healing and transformation. Continue to express your gratitude to one another, recognize and acknowledge the magnificence in each other. Your movie "Avatar" touched the hearts of millions because it resonated with the truth that each of you carry. Be mindful when you look at another, celebrate them and honor them for all they represent in the collective. Remember the phrase used in the movie, "I see you." When you say this to one another, either silently or aloud, you activate their own remembrance of oneness with the collective and the remembrance of who they are as divine beings of love.

WE SEE YOU! And we celebrate your brightness and your courage to walk this time frame and this dimension, offering your presence as a vehicle of evolution, healing and total transformation. Be in your joy and know that you are supported with this work and service that you offer to the collective through your personal awareness and experiences.

You! Yes, You!...
— March 2010

We greet you with great love and appreciation. We acknowledge your divine essence and magnificence. For far too long you have carried the disguise and the cloak of being unworthy, undeserving, not good enough, and inferior. We say this to you now, it is time to remove this disguise and honor yourself as the true magnificent, multidimensional being that you are.

Put aside any sense of inadequacy or imperfection. It matters not how these beliefs and judgments of self were acquired. It matters not the story that you tell yourself and others about your lack, or your limitations. You may experience some physical restrictions in your body, however, your most convincing and locked-down limitations are mental.

We invite you to consider these mental limitations as simply programs that have been activated by experiences you have encountered along the way. We will give you an example — just imagine for a moment that you had a defective program in your computer. You would delete this program and install new upgrades as soon as it was discovered. In other aspects of your reality, if it is broken, it is replaced or repaired.

Yet, we have observed your attachment to your personal limitations. Many individuals wear their restrictions like a badge, holding this frequency and silently saying to self and others, "I cannot possibly do that because I am unworthy. I am too ashamed, embarrassed, too shy, uneducated or inexperienced to ever claim my true power and worthiness."

We invite you to look within and ferret out any limitations that you might own, any limitations that are stopping you from stepping into your true nature as a divine being. Be the detective; watch your thoughts and actions for awhile, and you will discover the hidden inner beliefs that are stopping you from owning your power and purpose.

We remind you that you are not your physical vehicle. You are a being of LIGHT, pure energy and frequency. You are celestial; the essence of who you are is divine in nature, the spark, the connection of the All-That-Is, the holiest of holy.

You are a magnificent, multidimensional spark of the divine. Who you are in your physical guise is only one aspect of the great and grand, multidimensional matrix of who you truly are.

The time is now for you to claim this LIGHT, to own your unique gifts and offerings that add to the uplifting of consciousness on your planet. It is time to recognize and acknowledge who you are. It is time for you to accept and appreciate your personal dynamic vitality and influence upon the collective.

YOU! Yes, YOU are an important part of the transformation and the evolution that is taking place at this time.

When you own your authority of spirit, when you recognize that your thoughts, actions, and words are being added to the collective matrix, you begin to offer the vibrations and frequencies that uplift and heal.

You can use your prayers, your visions and your actions to enhance a more loving and forgiving reality. You acknowledge yourself and you acknowledge the other. You live from your heart lovingly and consciously, with the gentle awareness that you are contributing to the LIGHT of your world.

We acknowledge you in all your wonder, grace and radiance. Be embraced by our love and gratitude.

Powerful Alchemical Process...
— April 2010

We greet you with our love and gratitude. We embrace you with our acknowledgment for the courage and the integrity with which you are meeting your challenges. These are the changing times, these are the ending of cycles, and these are the times of great chaos. The levels of dysfunction are being unveiled and confirmed.

All that has been held in the shadows, all that is not in integrity, all that has been hidden, is being revealed. Secrecy and deceit can no longer be concealed. It is the light shining in these dark places within the collective consciousness that is pushing all to the surface of awareness. This is generating much fear and anxiety in the collective consciousness.

Yet, we say to you that these are also times of great celebration, these are times of incredible expansion and awakening within each individual. It is your light that is coming forth. It is your personal awakening that is to be celebrated.

You are here to support the transformation and the evolution of consciousness. You are an important aspect of all that is unfolding before you. You are far more powerful than you realize. We are here to remind you of your personal power and ability to uplift and transform dense, dysfunctional energy.

Resistance to the changes and the shift that are taking place will only cause more distress. When you are faced with great loss, do all within your power to offer your feelings of distress and fear up to be transformed.

This is the task you have come here to do, to transform the energies that do not support your well-being and the expansion. We invite you to give the feelings of discouragement, loss, fear or anger a voice, allow this act of release to be sacred.

Ask for support and see yourself surrounded by the love of divine consciousness, feel this embrace as you shout, weep, moan or scream your feelings. Give these feelings an expression in a sacred and holy way—honoring what you are feeling, yet being willing to allow them release and transformation. This is a powerful alchemical process.

When you offer a vibration that carries more light than darkness, you are adding to the expansion and the shift. When you recognize your own shadow issues and bring those to the light with understanding and forgiveness, you are doing global service work on a personal level.

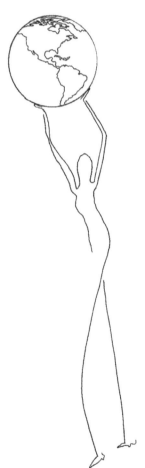

Your sacred heart is the vehicle of all transformation. When you consciously embrace an experience of fear with even the smallest shift of vibration into trust or hope, you own your power. Each and every time you consciously initiate a new response, you open the door to more light and claim more of your personal power.

Remember, you are a transformer. Step into your magnificence and own the ability to make a difference in each moment. Remember you are the one who carries the vision. You are the one who seeds your reality with your deepest knowing of truth and light.

You are here to anchor the new reality and the new shift of consciousness in the collective. It is within your heart chalice that the vision of love and peace will be anchored and brought forth.

Become a Stabilizer and Anchor...
—May, 2010

We Are Here, and we honor you with our love and support. We invite you to take a deep breath, and settle into the core of your physical form. In doing this you become an anchor for transformation. You become a stabilizer of the chaos energies in the collective consciousness. These are challenging times and these are times of great opportunities. When you anchor and stabilize, you claim your power to make a difference in what is occurring on the planet. It is time to claim and own your true magnificence and power.

When you observe the out-picturing of some occurrence, whether it is man made or a natural disaster, this is the time to immediately focus your energy and intention in the resolve and the support of those who are experiencing the tragic event. You are not a helpless observer. You are a part of the solution and the resolution.

This is the time for you to step forward in consciousness and know that you energetically join others who are also stepping forward to welcome a different reality. Your thoughts, emotions and intentions are the energetic tools that you offer in partnership with others, in partnership with the elements of nature, and in partnership with the consciousness of the planet that begins to create a shift in the outcome. Energetically joining this collective matrix of consciousness supports and assists the uplifting, healing and transformation of the chaos.

Know that, without a doubt, when you hold a vision of a better solution, when you imprint the quantum field of energy with more light, forgiveness and love, there will be a different result. This is true for what you are personally experiencing, and it is also true for the larger collective reality that you witness.

These are the opportunities that are before you. It is by stepping into your power, and stepping into your absolute knowing, that you are affecting the end results of any situation as a divine creator. When you realize you have an

154

active and personal role in the evolutionary shift occurring in the collective consciousness of humanity, you are powerful beyond measure.

Each moment in your life offers an opportunity to raise your vibrations, adding your coherent frequency of love, joy, gratitude and appreciate to the whole. We are aware that this exercise in consciousness is most difficult, especially when you are witnessing natural disasters around the world, as well as experiencing the personal adversity of job losses, health problems and family dynamics. The key is to know that you are not the victim of these circumstances, which in itself is an incredible shift of consciousness and awareness.

Practice mentally, emotionally and visually joining others energetically in the quantum field of all possibilities. Call upon the divine powers that be, the celestial realms, the angels and the elementals to assist and support the resolve of the various natural and man-made catastrophes that occur. Hold the vision of safety, and divine outcome for the good of all. Work consciously in the non-physical realms of energy to bring the perfect healing, the perfect solution, and the perfect resolve to all situations that you focus upon.

From your sacred heart awareness, engage the power of your energy, engage the power of prayers; use the power and expression of sound to release any emotional expression, either personal or in the collective; give a voice to the pain, sadness and fear that you or the collective is experiencing. When this exercise is done as a sacred and holy act, it will transform what is being held in the personal or collective emotional energy field. Replace what you have released with the intention and quality of something better and more expanded.

Be mindful to allow yourself grace in facing these challenges. Know that divine support is ever available upon request. Call upon this assistance at all times. Invite divine presence to work through you in all your actions. Become the anchor, the stabilizer of LIGHT and TRUTH in all circumstances. Allow yourself to feel our embrace of gratitude as you step into your true magnificence and power to invoke change.

Your future Self...

Every person is holding onto their collective reality, with its beliefs, projections, insecurities, hopes, dreams and desires. The view would be entirely expanded if the door of consciousness was fully opened, and all could see that the separate realities emerge from the same source, the grand truth of the oneness of all.

It is from your multidimensional perspective that you view the realities here on your planet. It is from the open door that you see or sense the grand truth. This earth is only one of the playgrounds in the galaxy, yet as humans, your focus is only in your small personal sandbox.

This is shifting. The aspect of you that knows the grand truth is stirring and awakening.

This is the energetic, evolutionary wave that is occurring in the psyche of all earth dwellers at this time. There are those who know and recognize their future self. They are aware of this aspect and are running to meet thier future self. There are many that have no idea that their future self exists in another timeframe or in another dimension.

It is the future self coming toward you, inviting you, beckoning you to merge, join and become fully aware of your magnificent, expanded, grand, multidimensional self.

In order to embrace or recognize any aspect of your unlimited self, you are invited to release the mental and emotional hold of the ego. You are invited to release the old patterns, any aspect of you that has served you up until this time, yet has locked you in the death grip of limitations.

When you practice holding a clear vibration of joy, gratitude and appreciation, you begin to soften the control of the ego mind. When you bless rather than judge, you soften the grip of the ego mind.

When you constantly remind yourself to place your awareness in your heart, you are softening the grip of your limited self. Each conscious act you practice is a step closer to your future self, the future self that is also walking toward you.

There will be a day in which you will embrace that future self and merge into the realms of unlimited wonder; you will emerge into your more expanded, multidimensional magnificence. We invite you to continue to take conscious steps forward, welcoming your future self. Relax, knowing that all is well, and you are loved and appreciated.

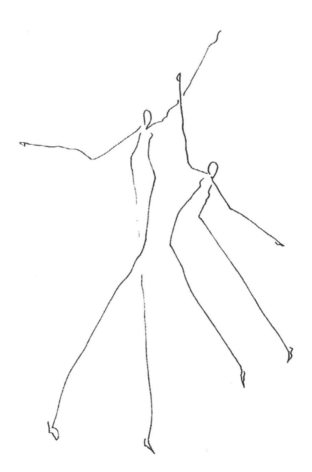

About the Author...

Peggy Black, Transducer, Scribe and Witness, is a world traveler and lecturer with thirty-five years experience in the healing field. She has been featured internationally in television, radio and print media. Peggy is a Multidimensional Channel whose gifts as a clairsentient, clairvoyant and clairaudient intuitive allow her to assist individuals to live empowered and abundant lives. Peggy receives transmissions from her "celestial team" which she calls the Morning Messages, inviting us to honor our multidimensional Self.

Sacred Sound Salutarist, Peggy uses powerful core sounds for vibrational healing. She is passionate about sharing the power of sound as a healing modality. She founded Sound Pod, and continues to create global community Sound Pods that empower others to freely use sound. She believes consciously intended sounds relieve stress, clear blockages and elevate awareness, promoting wholeness and healing.

Spiritual Synergist, she conducts ceremonies of transformation worldwide. Arabia, England, Ireland, Egypt, Japan and St. Lucia are a few of the sacred sites where ceremonies have been performed using the power of sound and the holiness of water. Peggy is the Seneschal for the Labyrinth in the Garden of the Beloved.

Peggy has presented at numerous events and conferences including Women of Vision and Action, Healing Our World, Kauai Wellness Expo, New England Sound Healing, World Sound Healing, and Global Sound. Peggy founded the International Sound Symposium. She offered sacred sounds for the Shamanic Journey tour in temples and the Great Pyramid in Egypt. She conducted morning forums at Tom Kenyon's Sound Healer's Trainings. She was Ceremonialist for the sacred water ceremony, Ocean of Gratitude Cruise with Dr. Masaru Emoto. She was featured in People magazine as "Fabulous over Sixty."

Peggy offers lectures and workshops: Miracles, Intentions and Manifestations, Allowing Prosperity, Sound Awareness, Sculpting Reality with Sound, The Power of Your Words and Intentions, The Creative You, and Engaging Celestial Support.

Peggy still lives in the home she built in the redwoods near Santa Cruz, CA. Contact her at www.peggyblack.com.

Acknowledgment and Support...

Motivational Press:
    Justin Sachs, www.Motivationalpress.com
Graphic Art and Design:
    Melanie Gendron, www.melaniegendron.com
C&C Offset Printing Company:
    Vicki Lundgren, www.ccoffset.com
Intention Partner:
    New Perspectives, Ellen Henson, Ellen@lifeInsights.net
Intention Partner:
    Susanne Craig
Office Goddess:
    Nicole Morelli
Editing Support:
    Jennifer Grady
Editing Support:
    Tom Johnson and Michael Ruggles
Founder of Author One Stop:
    Randy Peyser, www.AuthorOneStop.com
Founder of Share Foundation and S.E.E Publishing:
    Virginia Essene, www.virginiaessene.com
Founder of The Angel Ministry:
    Rev. Kimberly Marooney, Ph.D www.TheAngelMinistry.com
Glimpse into Another Reality:
    Barbara Thomas, www.barbarathomas.info
Cosmic Telepath:
    Ronna Herman, www.AskArchangelMichael.com
Marketing:
    Peter Melton, author of *Waves of Oneness*

The companion book, *The Morning Messages "We Are Here" Transmissions*, includes credits for all who supported the projects and offerings of Morning Messages.

The assistance and encouragement of these many friends and professionals is deeply appreciated; their energy directly and indirectly nurtures this book as well. I am grateful for our continuing partnership.

Kudos for Personal Channeled Transmissions...

I was elated by our session that you so magically and brilliantly organized for me. The visionary direction for my personal growth and to bring about the "shift" in consciousness was remarkable. This was the best and most inspiring psychic reading I have ever had. — Blessings, Luise

I sit in a space of wondrous gratitude and appreciation for the amazing gift I have been bestowed. The session I had with you and your team touched me to the very depths of my soul and I am changed and transformed forever. You and your team are amazing. — Trish

Hello, dearest Peggy, WOW, was that ever a fantastic experience. I had no idea I would realize so much in one call. You facilitated so much for me and I am so grateful. Your support and love was as healing as all of it. I had the best day with my Beloved after that call, and felt freer than I have in several months. — Thank you, Kent

I am seeing so clearly and with great understanding. I am so thankful I had this session. I remember when they said they were going to open circuits, well, I am feeling as if doors are opening and I can feel I am expanding. It is wonderful. — Dianne

Thank you for such a powerful, healing, transformative experience! This reading felt different, the energetic transmission of Light was palpable, so comforting and affirming. I was deeply affected by the healing and uplifting energy, I feel renewed. — Kathy

Thank you Peggy for the transforming experience; it was practical and inspirational all at the same time. The important confusing questions were answered plainly and honestly. I feel encouraged to go ahead with all my plans. I feel completely free of doubts that were making me sad and afraid. I am grateful forever. — Love, Dolores

Hi Peggy, It was good connecting with you and the Team this afternoon. I've got a more balanced perspective now and I'm feeling much improved. I wanted to thank you for your part in the session, as your warmth and understanding made a big difference in assisting me to move forward. — Very best regards, Michael

Kudos for Products...

I hesitated to buy the CD at the time, and I would like to encourage anyone that has any doubts to please take the risk as they will never regret their choice to be surrounded by the loving energy. No matter how many times I listen to your "friends" I feel the freshness of them speaking to my heart. Their love and light comes through with each hearing for me and seems to be extended to others who I meet without saying a word. — A most affectionate HUG across the place beyond time and distance, Gail

Your CD of daily messages has been my constant companion when driving my car. I am extremely grateful for their words... it helps me refocus my "mind Chatter." Written or spoken, the messages are very much appreciated. — Joanie.

Unknowingly, you have been instrumental in my new and expanded experience. I use my Morning Messages deck of cards daily and the messages are right on. They resonate with insights of wisdom and guidance to a conscious life. — Thanks, Marlon

I love to hold these precious cards to my heart, while I say a prayer to Source and my team. I enjoy using the message as a mantra "I AM a tranformer!" throughout my day. The beautiful image of the card is a wonderful visual connection with my team and their immense love that is always here for me! — Michelle

I listen to the Morning Messages CD each night as I fall asleep; if I wake in the middle of the night, I play them again. I find these words inspiring and expanding. — Bless you, Marylou

Each morning after my meditation, I pull one of your invitation cards from the beautiful Morning Messages Invitations deck, and it helps me remember that I am a spiritual being living this life as I head out the door to work. I have brought them to staff meetings and everyone enjoyed their message. — Debbie

The morning messages deck gives me inspiration in living my life in a state of remembrance and gratitude and joy as well as being a wonderful source of counsel and encouragement on specific issues. — Susana

More Offerings from Morning Messages...

Morning Messages "We Are Here" Transmissions Book includes the unfolding, miraculous story of the process and eighty-eight illustrated messages. These messages open new doors and bust down some of your old doors and beliefs. Each message will intrigue and invite you to practice fresh ways of looking at your life.

Morning Messages Invitations Book—forty-four invitations that will entice and summon you to step into a new way of responding to your life. Once you begin using these invitations, there will be no turning back. Your life will change. Your life will transform. You will begin to expect miracles every day.

"We Are Here" Transmissions, the Morning Messages—Double CD Set—The Audio version of the Morning Messages will give you a quick, vibrational frequency boost. Listen in the car, on the plane, as a meditation, when you need to remember your magnificence, or to maintain your high frequency of joy, gratitude and appreciation.

The Morning Messages Invitation Deck—44 invitations offering consciousness exercises to support your well-being and expansion.

Celebrating the Morning Messages—DVD, 50 minute presentation: The Story, Heart Space, Celestial Partnership

Wisdom and Guidelines for Multidimensional Humans Poster
These eleven guidelines inspire and uplift. They offer a focus to shift our consciousness. They encourage us to remember that our thoughts, words, deeds and actions affect the whole.

Other 8.5x11 Inspirational Posters Available on Web Site

Join the Morning Message family—subscribe for the free 88 messages: www.morningmessages.com.

Peggy is available for personal channeled transmissions, lectures and workshops. These channeled readings offer insights and guidance to bring clarity to your personal challenges and questions—joyandgratitude@aol.com.

For information or inquiries about wholesale purchases, contact Peggy Black, 831-335-3145, or peggyblack@aol.com.

CPSIA information can be obtained at www.ICGtesting.com
Printed in the USA
BVOW11s2017280514

354598BV00011B/187/P